YOUR GUIDE TO
VIDEO GAME LIVESTREAMING

GAMING
LIVE!

EDITOR IN CHIEF
Ryan King

EDITOR
Stephen Ashby

WRITERS
Vikki Blake, Wesley Copeland, Jason Fanelli, Barry Keating, Carrie Mok, Dominic Reseigh-Lincoln, John Robertson, Edward Smith

LEAD DESIGNER
Greg Whitaker

DESIGNERS
Abbi Castle, Steve Dacombe, Andy Downes, Ali Innes, Adam Markiewicz, Anne-Claire Pickard, Andy Salter, Will Shum, Sophie Ward, Perry Wardell-Wicks

PRODUCTION
Sanne de Boer, Ross Hamilton, Phil King, Carrie Mok, Philip Morris, Jen Neal, Rebecca Richards, Hannah Westlake, Jon White

ISBN 978-1-3380-3273-4
10 9 8 7 6 5 4 3 2 1   16 17 18 19
Printed in the U.S.A. 40
First printing, September 2016

Scholastic is constantly working to lessen the environmental impact of our manufacturing processes. To view our industry-leading paper procurement policy, visit www.scholastic.com/paperpolicy.

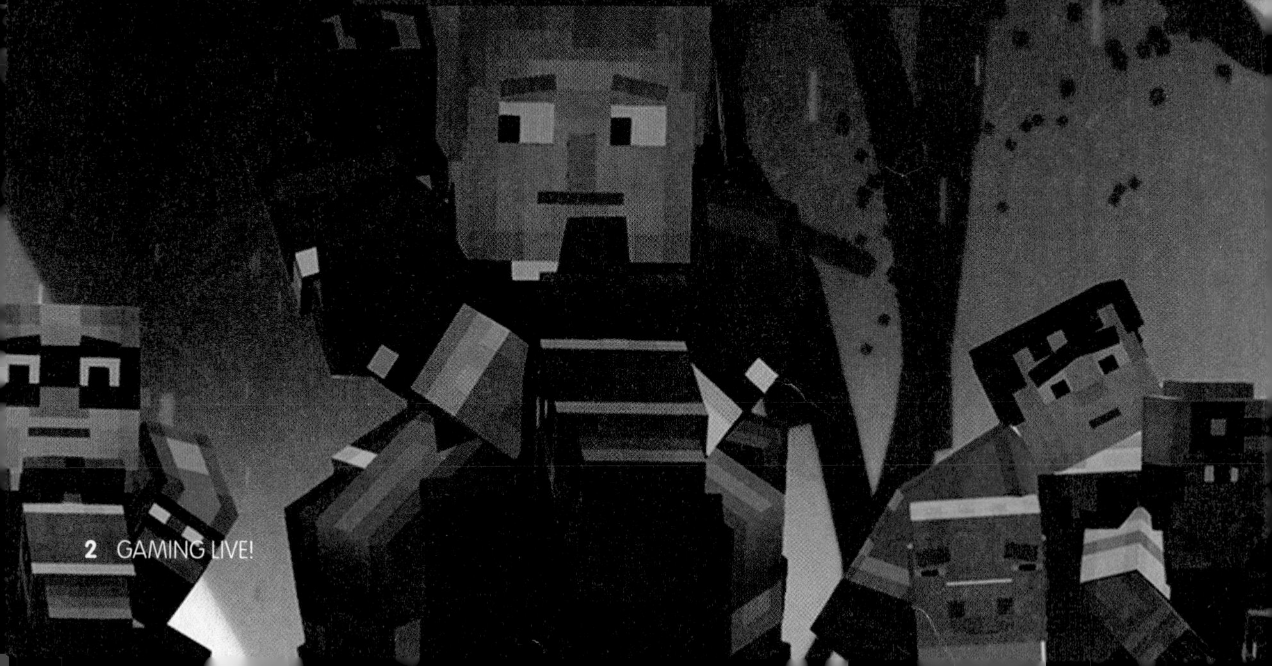

MINECRAFT: STORY MODE

A TELLTALE GAMES SERIES

Minecraft: Story Mode took the world by storm when it was released, and it has quickly become one of the most popular games for Let's Players!

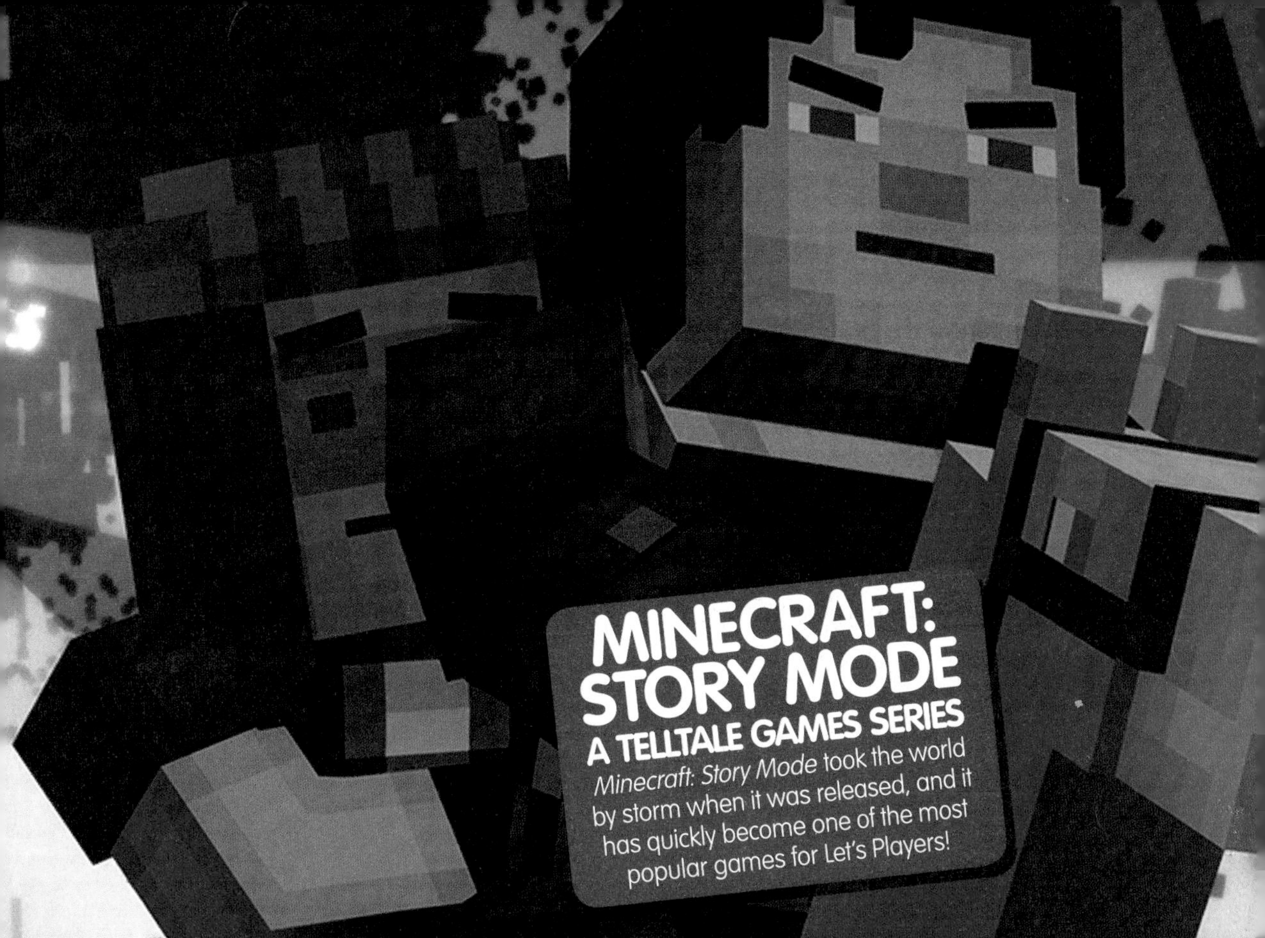

STAYING SAFE AND HAVING FUN

Always check out a game's rating before you play it. The ratings are there for a reason, not to stop you from having fun. If you're playing online with others, remember that they're not real-life friends. Here are 12 tips for staying safe when you're gaming online:

1 Talk to your parents about your family's rules regarding how long you can stay online, what websites you can visit on the Internet, and what you can and can't do.

2 Don't give out any of your passwords to anyone other than your parents.

3 Never give out personal information such as your real name, phone number, or anything about your parents.

4 Never agree to meet in person with someone you met online.

5 Tell your parents or a teacher if you come across anything that makes you feel uncomfortable when you're online.

6 Don't feel pressured into giving any money to anyone online for subscriptions to their channel or donations to their work. It's totally optional and you can still enjoy their content without paying a penny.

7 The world of livestreaming is always changing. If any video, conversation or comment makes you feel uncomfortable, just close the page. There are plenty more streamers to choose from!

8 Don't download or install software, games, or apps to any console or device, or fill out any forms on the Internet, without first checking with the person that the device you're using belongs to.

9 Don't post pictures your parents might think are inappropriate. Anything you post can be seen by anyone and for a long time, so be careful.

10 When you're online, be nice to other people. Don't say or do anything that could hurt someone else's feelings or make them feel unhappy.

11 Don't respond to any conversations that are mean or make you feel bad. It's not your fault if someone sends you something bad. Let your parents know right away.

12 Video games are the most amazing things ever! Let everyone know how to have fun playing online, safely.

CONTENTS

TIPS & TRICKS

INSIDER ACCESS

WELCOME TO GAMING LIVE!

THE ULTIMATE GUIDE TO STREAMING AND LET'S PLAYS!

Gaming in 2017 is about more than just picking up a pad and playing your favorite game with friends. That's really fun and we're all still doing it, but sometimes you just want to kick back, put your controller down, and watch someone else do the hard work.

You can watch all kinds of games online, from professional eSports gamers playing *League of Legends* in massive stadiums to people beating *Garden Warfare 2* in their bedrooms for fun. In this book, we'll take you through the most popular titles, and give you behind-the-scenes access to the stars of streaming.

Whether you're subscribed to dozens of channels or have just watched your very first Let's Play, this book is packed full of action that will inspire, surprise, and amaze you. Gaming has changed a lot in the last few years, but read on and you'll soon be ahead of the curve in the biggest revolution the industry has ever seen …

54

Penny

One time I found a really old piece of pottery. It had
writing on it that I couldn't read.

WHAT IS LIVESTREAMING?

Livestreaming is, quite simply, broadcasting content as it happens. That's it! Millions of people around the world broadcast anything and everything live as it happens, and that includes gaming. You can see people put together crafty *Super Mario Maker* levels, and then challenge the world to beat their clever creations. You can watch the best players in the world battle it out at *Overwatch*, getting an exclusive inside view of the tricks and techniques they use, maybe even gaining insight into characters you never thought you would use. You can enjoy someone completing *Unravel* for the first time, giggling with delight at the charming surprises within and

stumbling onto secrets that even you haven't found yet. Best of all, you can see new games being played as soon as the wrapper has been torn off, so you'll know whether it's the right game for you before you decide to invest your time. Sometimes, you can even see games in action before they hit the shelves.

And make no mistake—whether it's gamers tuning in to watch experts at the peak of their powers, or those who entertain with their excessive reactions and hilarious running commentary, livestreaming is huge. Since Twitch kickstarted the livestreaming phenomenon in June 2011, there have been over 2 million broadcasters

showing their skills off to the world, and over 100 million people tune in every single month to watch. If those numbers aren't enough to make your eyes water, how about this—over 240 billion minutes of gaming have been broadcast to date. And it's not just Twitch—you can also watch broadcasts on YouTube Gaming, alongside the millions of other gaming videos that are already hosted and available to watch on YouTube.

Simply put, livestreaming is the biggest thing to happen to gaming in years, and if you want to enjoy the wide variety of games out there, along with the people who play them, this is the place to start!

BATCOMPUTER

BATMAN (THE BATMAN OF ZUR-EN

4/4

WHAT WAS THE BIGGEST MINECRAFT LIVESTREAM?

The BIGGEST Moments in Livestreaming ... EVER

WHEN DID PEWDIEPIE BEGIN HIS UNSTOPPABLE RISE?

WHEN DID YOUTUBE START?

HERE'S EVERY HUGE LIVESTREAMING AND YOUTUBE MOMENT, FROM THE BEGINNING RIGHT UP TO TODAY!

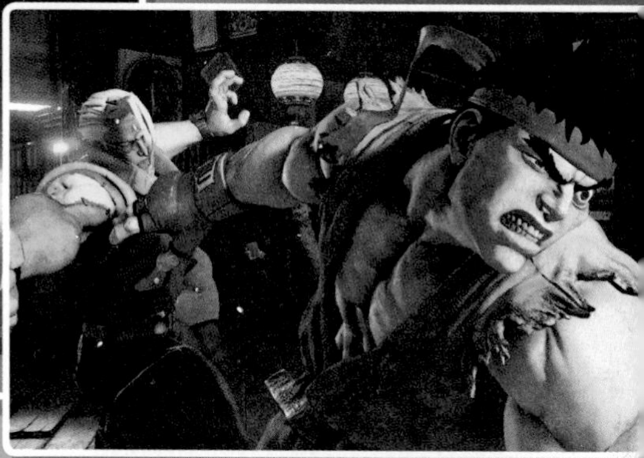

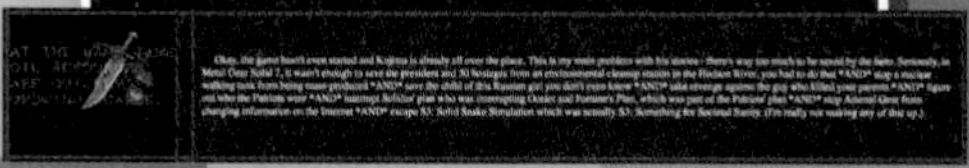

FEBRUARY 2005

THE BIRTH OF YOUTUBE

▶ YouTube is founded by three guys who want a way to share their cool videos with the world! There wasn't an easy way for gaming fans to share videos before YouTube, or even to find them. Gaming fans had to hope someone had the equipment to record videos—which was expensive and awkward to use back then—and a place to upload them.

APRIL 2005

YOUTUBE'S FIRST-EVER VIDEO

▶ The first ever video, "Me At The Zoo," is uploaded to YouTube on April 23. It's a 19-second video of one of YouTube's creators at San Diego Zoo. The first ever comment on that video, which is posted a month later, is "LOL!!!!!!".

AUGUST 2004

THE FIRST LET'S PLAY?

▶ Commentating on games while playing through them wasn't called "Let's Play" when the idea first started. One of the earliest examples comes from "Slowbeef," who posts a *Metal Gear 2: Solid Snake* playthrough on his personal website with text commentary accompanying screenshots. The funny observations and witty commentary while playing through the game will go on to become hallmarks of modern Let's Play videos.

OCTOBER 2005

LET'S PLAY BEGINS!

▶ In late 2005, sometime around October, the first forum thread to popularize the "Let's Play" movement is born on the Something Awful forums. The game is *Oregon Trail* and the thread is called, unsurprisingly, Let's Play Oregon Trail. Forum members volunteer themselves to be part of the traveling party in the game, offering strategies, suggesting what to do, and contributing text commentary as the game progresses through screenshots that show updates. The name "Let's Play" comes from the fact that they are all playing *Oregon Trail* together! The thread has since been lost to time but after the initial success of Let's Play Oregon Trail, several other Let's Play threads appeared on the Something Awful forums for games like *Final Fantasy VI*.

DECEMBER 2005

THE FIRST POPULAR GAMING VIDEO TAKES OFF

▶ YouTube user "foolished" uploads a video of the battle between Justin Wong and Daigo from the *Street Fighter III: 3rd Strike* semifinals, taken from the international gaming tournament Evolution Championship Series in 2004. The moment when Daigo mounts a stunning comeback, with the crowd cheering on his victory, has been widely talked about on forums and niche websites in the years since it happened. But now, with YouTube hosting the video, there is a home where everyone can access it, and it remains one of the most important and influential gaming videos of all time, having amassed over 5 million views.

APRIL 2011

PEWDIEPIE JOINS YOUTUBE

▶ After forgetting the password to his original account, Swedish university student Felix Kjellberg creates a new YouTube account called PewDiePie and starts uploading gaming videos. He would go on to become YouTube's biggest ever star.

JUNE 2011

TWITCH BEGINS!

▶ The gaming side of Justin.tv has outgrown its original home and is separated into its own site, Twitch.tv. While Justin.tv let its users broadcast anything and everything (within reason!), Twitch focuses on games and games alone. Playthroughs of games and broadcasts of eSports competitions prove particularly popular.

JULY 2011

STAMPYLONGHEAD JOINS YOUTUBE

▶ As part of his video production course in college, and with an eye toward becoming a games journalist, Joseph Garrett joins YouTube as stampylonghead.

APRIL 2006

SMOSH BECOMES THE VERY BEST

▶ One of the earliest YouTube gaming channels, Smosh earns fame as a lip-syncing take on *Pokémon*'s theme song hits 24 million views, becoming the most viewed video on YouTube at that time. For copyright reasons, though, YouTube had to remove the video.

POKEMON!

JANUARY 2007

LET'S PLAY WITH VIDEOS

▶ An important livestreaming milestone happens on the Something Awful forums when Slowbeef switches to a video format during his Let's Play of old retro game *The Immortal*. The video format is really well received and sets the template for Let's Play installments in the years to come.

DID YOU KNOW?

You can Like your favorite streamers on Facebook so you get alerts when they stream live or add a new video!

MAY 2009

MINECRAFT IS FIRST RELEASED

▶ Markus "Notch" Persson releases *Minecraft* on forums for developers. He also uploads a video to his YouTube channel showcasing the interactive mobs and terrain, marking the first ever *Minecraft* video on YouTube. It certainly wasn't the last …

MARCH 2007

THE (UNOFFICIAL) START OF TWITCH

▶ Four guys get together in San Francisco and launch Justin.tv, which lets users broadcast whatever they want, whenever they want … within reason, of course! There are different categories that people can choose from on Justin.tv, including gaming, where users play through their most-loved games. This gaming channel would eventually become Twitch.

NOVEMBER 2011

DREAMHACK AND TWITCH TEAM UP

▶ The first huge victory for Twitch.tv happens just a few months after separating from Justin.tv, when DreamHack Winter 2011 is broadcast to 1.7 million individual viewers on the site. It isn't just an important milestone for Twitch.tv, which finds itself the go-to place for fans wanting to watch the *StarCraft II: Wings of Liberty* main event, it also helps to establish DreamHack as one of the biggest gaming tournaments in the world.

AUGUST 2013

PEWDIEPIE LEADS YOUTUBE

▶ Just over two years after creating his account, PewDiePie becomes the biggest YouTuber in theworld, overtaking the likes of Smosh, CaptainSparklez and TheDiamondMinecart.

MARCH 2014

TWITCH PLAYS POKÉMON ENDS

▶ After 16 days of endless gameplay, Twitch completes *Pokémon Red*. Over a million players have taken part, with 55 million views. The popularity of the experiment leads to the creation of an entire sub-genre of "TwitchPlays." The strangest idea? "FishPlaysStreetFighter," where the positions of two fish in a tank determine what special moves happen in *Street Fighter II* … it may sound strange but it's compelling viewing!

FEBRUARY 2014

TWITCH PLAYS POKÉMON STARTS

▶ A new channel appears on Twitch called TwitchPlaysPokemon. Started as a social experiment, this Twitch channel displays Game Boy classic *Pokémon Red*, with Twitch viewers able to control the on-screen action by typing Up, Down, Left, Right, A, B, Select, and Start. The problem? *Every* Twitch player can affect the gameplay … so imagine the absolute chaos when 120,000 viewers attempt to play the game at the same time!

SEPTEMBER 2013

THAT SINKING FEELING …

▶ Stampylonghead uploads "Sinking Feeling," one of his many Let's Play videos for *Minecraft* on Xbox 360. This 23-minute video proves to be extremely popular and goes on to become one of the biggest Let's Play videos on YouTube, with over 44 million views!

OCTOBER 2013

LEAGUE OF LEGENDS BREAKS RECORDS

▶ Shortly after the *League Of Legends* Season 3 World Championship comes to a close, Riot Games claims that it is "the most watched eSports event in history" with 32 million fans watching on Twitch. The year before, Season 2 World Championship was watched by 8.2 million fans.

JUNE 2014

NINTENDO JOINS IN

▶ Nintendo had been focusing on making amazing games, but eventually it couldn't resist joining in. At its Electronic Entertainment Expo (E3) press conference in 2014, Nintendo hosted an invitational tournament for Super Smash Bros on Wii U. It streamed the tournament through Twitch, with ZeRo's Zero Suit Samus defeating Hungrybox's Kirby in the grand final.

AUGUST 2014

SKATE 3 RE-CHARTS

Four-year-old game *Skate 3* is propelled back up the charts due to its use in numerous comedy videos from prominent YouTubers.

MARCH 2015

YOUTUBE RELAUNCHES LIVESTREAMING

▶ Twitch had established itself firmly as the place to watch people gaming live, but YouTube wanted in on the action. So the Google-owned company relaunches its Live section, with a focus on eSports events, gaming conventions, and other big draws for gaming audiences. As it turned out, this was only the start of YouTube's assault on Twitch ...

JUNE 2015

LARGEST MINECRAFT PIXEL ART EVER

▶ Streamer Thorlar has spent 23 weeks on Twitch creating the biggest pixel-art image ever made in *Minecraft*. Having made previous pixel-art pictures in the game, and based on his viewers saying that they had never seen images as big as his, he decided to go for broke ... the final picture weighs in at a staggering 1,128,960 blocks! Even better, the ad revenue generated by the stream is donated to the Make-A-Wish Ireland charity!

AUGUST 2015

YOUTUBE GAMING LAUNCHES

▶ Gaming videos on YouTube become so popular that YouTube decides to launch YouTube Gaming, a spin-off channel to follow the success of its livestreaming relaunch in March 2015.

FEBRUARY 2016

WATCH TWITCH, EARN REWARDS

▶ Twitch and Blizzard quietly joined forces in September 2015 and *Heroes Of The Storm* benefits all this time later, as you could unlock two Heroes portraits just by watching Heroes tournaments on Twitch!

MARCH 2016

TWITCH GOES SUPER SOCIAL

▶ The Channel Feed beta launches! Which is the fancy way of saying Twitch now lets their users bring their Facebook, Twitter, and other social media profiles onto their Twitch channel.

WHO ARE THE COOLEST STREAMERS IN THE WORLD?

FANS
270,000+
KNOWN FOR
Good vibes and positivity!

FANS
2.1 million+
KNOWN FOR
Making League Of Legends!

RIOTGAMES

● Of course, Riot Games themselves have a Twitch channel, and it's packed with all sorts of *League Of Legends* action. It's naturally the first port of call to any *League Of Legends* fan and often where new characters will be showcased ahead of release.

DETHRIDGECRAFT

● DethridgeCraft loves getting stuck into a whole host of games, from *WWE 2K16* to *Stardew Valley* to *Minecraft*. But whatever he's playing, the chilled-out, positive attitude remains the same, and it's the main reason his fanbase grows by the day!

BIGGEST YOUTUBERS IN THE WORLD

FANS
11 million+
KNOWN FOR
Over-the-top reactions

FANS
12 million+
KNOWN FOR
Being one of the biggest YouTubers!

I LIKE MORE THAN SPACE

SKYDOESMINECRAFT

● Combining his endless creativity and love for *Minecraft*, SkyDoesMinecraft has become one of the most popular YouTubers in the world—every video brings something new.

MARKIPLIER

● Mark has now branched out into different gaming videos and is also becoming known for his charity work, but Markiplier's calling card will always be his ridiculous reactions!

NIGHT BLUE3

FANS
1.2 million+
KNOWN FOR
Informative League Of Legends streams

● This *League Of Legends* expert streams for around seven hours each day, and each stream is packed full of useful information, tips, and tricks to get ahead. He streams so much *League* content, even the biggest *League of Legends* fan will learn something new.

JULIA_TV

● Julia TV is one of best variety streamers out there, which means she plays a whole range of games—*Stardew Valley, Zelda: Wind Waker, The Sims 4,* and *Mario Kart 8* are recent examples. To see a host of different games, check her out!

FANS
72,000+
KNOWN FOR
Playing anything and everything

ITSHAFU

● One of the most knowledgable *Hearthstone* experts on Twitch, Hafu streams live for over ten hours a day … and on some occasions over 20 hours a day! Even so, Hafu is always upbeat, friendly, and welcoming to all her Twitch followers.

FANS
400,000+
KNOWN FOR
Hearthstone expertise

FANS
500,000+
KNOWN FOR
League of Legends dominance

FROGGEN

● *League Of Legends* pro Froggen is regarded as one of the best players in the world, so it's little wonder the Danish player's stream is so popular. Froggen is known for his Anivia play in *League of Legends* but even if you aren't a fan, he's worth watching to see a real gaming superstar in action.

FANS
9 million+
KNOWN FOR
His Minecraft gameplay

THEDIAMONDMINECART

● If you want to see *Minecraft* delivered with witty observations, hilarious humor and smart game play, make sure you watch Dan "TheDiamondMinecart" on YouTube.

FANS
8 million+
KNOWN FOR
His explosive energy

JACKSEPTICEYE

● Is there anyone anywhere in the world with more energy than Jacksepticeye? Regardless of what game it is that he's playing, it's exhausting just trying to keep up with him!

TOYS COME TO LIFE
SKYLANDERS

There's a reason why *Skylanders* is so popular with gamers—the first major toys-to-life game to land on consoles was also one of the best, with great level design and cool toys combining into an enjoyable and unique experience. A few years on, and *Skylanders* is still a massive franchise, and the games have just got better and better.

And as you might expect, the series has amassed quite a following, both offline and on the Internet. Dedicated channels have been set up to document the latest character releases and game levels, and they really know their stuff. Whether you've played the action platformer before or are just buying your first figures, these are the channels to tune into if you want to get some great advice.

DID YOU KNOW?
The biggest *Skylanders* collection consists of 4,100 unique items and earned its owner a Guinness World Record.

STREAMERS' TOP TIPS

SEARCH FOR COLLECTIBLES
Whether it's coins you can spend on improving your character, or Stardust for boosting your Portal Master Rank, *Skylanders* games are full of useful trinkets for you to find.

USE ALL YOUR FIGURES
You'll probably get new Starter Pack figures when you buy a new game, but you can still use your old toys in the new titles. So make sure you don't throw them away.

LEVEL UP FAST
If you want to level up fast in *Skylanders Superchargers*, head over to Battle Brawl Island. Fight your way through the arena and defeat the likes of Captain Bristlestache for lots of experience.

GET FANCY
Make sure that you equip the hats that you find on your Skylanders. Hats give your character a bonus, such as increased armor, a higher critical hit chance, or improved speed.

BIGGEST YOUTUBERS

SKYLANDER BOY AND GIRL
NAME: MICHAEL, CHASE, AND LEXI
● NO. OF FOLLOWERS: 1,080,000
● NO. OF VIEWS: 1,240,000,000

ABOUT: This family of gamers love playing together—whether it's mum and dad facing off against each other, the kids explaining tricks and tips, or the whole family performing skits and games together. They really know their stuff when it comes to *Skylanders*, so you can always get good advice from their channel. Best of all, they have a series of animated shorts featuring the Skylanders themselves!

HILARIOUSNESS	4
TALKATIVENESS	5
KNOWLEDGE	3
COLLECTION	5
SKILL	3

JASON INQUIRES
NAME: JASON GRIER
● NO. OF FOLLOWERS: 2,500 ● NO. OF VIEWS: 110,000

ABOUT: Jason's channel covers every single toys-to-life franchise you care to name, making him *the* place to go to get your *Skylanders* knowledge. Regular news updates will help you stay up to date with the new releases and game news for your favorite franchise, and his unboxing videos are always packed with useful information.

HILARIOUSNESS	2
TALKATIVENESS	4
KNOWLEDGE	5
COLLECTION	5
SKILL	4

1OFWIISDOM
NAME: UNKNOWN
● NO. OF FOLLOWERS: 8,700 ● NO. OF VIEWS: 10,800,000

ABOUT: This portal master is a great resource when it comes to statistics for in-game characters. He logs attack damage, critical damage, and more during his chilled out videos, which will help you decide on the best Skylanders to choose for each new mission. He also covers new characters as they're released

HILARIOUSNESS	
TALKATIVENESS	3
KNOWLEDGE	5
COLLECTION	4
SKILL	5

MALICEDOLL79
NAME: UNKNOWN
● NO. OF FOLLOWERS: 10,000 ● NO. OF VIEWS: 7,000,000

ABOUT: From unboxings of the latest figures to gameplay videos and races, MALICEDOLL79 packs a lot of *Skylanders* content into his channel. He covers other games, too, including other toys-to-life titles, but he really knows his stuff when it comes to *Skylanders*. His demos of the latest toys are especially good, as he analyses their strengths and weaknesses.

HILARIOUSNESS	3
TALKATIVENESS	4
KNOWLEDGE	5
COLLECTION	5
SKILL	4

EVANTUBEHD
● NO. OF FOLLOWERS: 2,900,000 ● NO. OF VIEWS: 2,000,000,000

ABOUT: Evan always has a smile on his face—which is understandable when you're a 10-year-old kid surrounded by figurines! He reviews all kinds of things on his channel, from toys-to-life figures to plain old toys. There isn't much gameplay here, but if you're more interested in the toys than the game, this is the channel for you.

HILARIOUSNESS	3
TALKATIVENESS	5
KNOWLEDGE	4
COLLECTION	4
SKILL	2

GET IN YOUR LANE

LEAGUE OF LEGENDS

No game in eSports can match *League of Legends* in popularity. The MOBA has almost 70 million monthly players, and more than 30 million people tune into the competitive world finals each year—that's more than the World Series in America! The pro players that take part in these competitions don't only play on the pro circuit, though—many sharpen their skills while streaming on Twitch and YouTube.

These outlets are hugely popular, too, with many of the pros now boasting over a million subscribers each. If you've just started watching *League* online, these guys can help you pick up the basics. Or, if you already know your Junglers from your Bottom Laners, studying how the pros play will help you take your own skills to the next level. Whatever your experience, these are the guys to help you up your game, so tune in!

TOP 3 STREAM MOMENTS

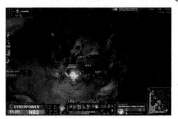

THE LONGEST PENTAKILL
MARCH 10, 2015

1 When Doublelift was playing with the CLG Squad, his team camped the enemy base trying to take out all five opponents at once to get a 'pentakill.' Something went wrong, and Doublelift got only four kills, but somehow a respawn kill got him his penta—despite being several seconds later. When the notification finally appeared, everyone went crazy.

DANCE PARTY!
OCTOBER 2, 2015

2 Bjergsen is pretty chill when it comes to playing online, which is why he often makes his character dance with enemies and teammates alike. As they partied out, Bjerg opened YouTube to drop a beat. But the opposition player stopped dancing just as the song kicked in—so Bjerg instantly killed him.

THE KILL THIEF
JANUARY 15, 2015

3 While NightBlue3 spends a lot of his time giving advice, he also takes any chances he can. In this highlight, he sees the enemy team attacking a dragon and uses his jump attack to leap into the fray at the very last second and steal the kill from the opponents without them even noticing he's there. Sneaky!

STREAMERS' TOP CHARACTER PICKS

MAOKAI

STREAMER: TheOddOne **PRIMARY ROLE:** Tank

LEVELS
ATTACK: **3** DEFENSE: **8** ABILITY: **6** DIFFICULTY: **3**

WHY THEM? Maokai suits TheOddOne's jungling preference, as his Sapling Toss and Arcane Smash abilities do a great job of clearing the jungle quickly. He often starts with Hunter's Machete and Health Potion as his items to increase his damage against large monsters and help him stay alive longer.

ABILITIES

| SAP MAGIC | ARCANE SMASH | VENGEFUL MAELSTROM | SAPLING TOSS | TWISTED ADVANCE |

KATARINA

STREAMER: Scarra
PRIMARY ROLE: Assassin

LEVELS
ATTACK: **4** DEFENSE: **3**
ABILITY: **9** DIFFICULTY: **8**

WHY THEM? Katarina is one of the few manaless champions and her abilities are based entirely on cooldowns, so Scarra uses a lot of spells while playing as her. She is capable of busting down multiple targets at a time, thanks to her great mobility and multi-target kit.

ABILITIES

VORACITY | BOUNCING BLADES | SINISTER STEEL | SHUNPO | DEATH LOTUS

YASUO

STREAMER: VoyBoy
PRIMARY ROLE: Fighter

LEVELS
ATTACK: **8** DEFENSE: **4** ABILITY: **4** DIFFICULTY: **10**

WHY THEM? Yasuo's damage output ramps up the longer he survives in combat, meaning VoyBoy plays a careful game of survival. He can only dish out low damage during Yasuo's early game, though, meaning the hero is more suited to mid-lane combat. Still, VoyBoy likes to play top-lane with Yasuo, which just shows how good he is at *League*.

ABILITIES

WAY OF THE WANDERER | STEEL TEMPEST | WIND WALL | SWEEPING BLADE | LAST BREATH

STREAMERS' TOP TIPS

LEARN TO WARD
Warding might seem like a waste of your gaming gold, but learn how to place them well (focus on the Jungle) and they'll give you and your team a massive advantage.

LAST HIT MINIONS
Last-hitting minions is a vital skill. Wait until your minions have worn the other team's minions down, and then attack to get the last hit, finishing them off and earning more gold.

SHARE TACTICS
Sharing tactics with your teammates is vital to success. Use the notifications system to tell your team what you're doing and when you need support, using the pre-written messages.

TEAM IS EVERYTHING
Always be ready to help out a teammate—if they're getting overrun in the mid-lane, hightail it there to lessen the load. If you go lone wolf you're basically going to lose.

ORE-SOME FUN!

MINECRAFT

When creator Markus "Notch" Persson first conceived the idea of a building game called *Cave Game*, no-one—not even Notch himself—could've suspected that the game we now know as *Minecraft* would become one of the most successful video games of all time.

Having sold over 70 million copies, and with thousands of people still populating every *Minecraft* server, the game's popularity shows no sign of slowing down. Whether you enjoy exploring the world, crafting shiny items, tending your farm animals, or just running around with your buddies, there's no denying that *Minecraft* has something to offer every type of gamer.

Thanks to the mobile versions available, you can carry your crafty world in your pocket too—the only limit to *Minecraft*'s immense possibilities is your own imagination and a Creeper or two …

TOP 3 LET'S PLAY MOMENTS

MINECRAFT— UNEXPECTED DRAMA
DECEMBER 8, 2012

1 Most of the time, *Stampy's Lovely World* YouTube series is exactly that—lovely! But when Hit The Target unexpectedly turns on Stampy, he's left with no alternative but to take the griefer on! In "Unexpected Drama," you can watch Stampy defeat Hit the Target and watch his nemesis's dungeon go up in flames!

THE SIMPSONS OPENING IN MINECRAFT
SEPTEMBER 25, 2011

2 There's a whole host of faithful re-creations of famous TV and movie scenes on YouTube, but this remake of *The Simpsons*' opening credits has to be one of our favorites. It has everything, from Bart writing lines on the school board to Lisa's band practise—there's even a couch gag! Check it out!

OCARINA OF TIME RE-CREATED IN MINECRAFT
NOVEMBER 12, 2010

3 Talking of re-creations … you have to check out NinBuzz's incredible re-creation of the Great Deku Tree dungeon from *The Legend of Zelda: Ocarina of Time*. With awesome attention to detail—there's a map, a compass, and even a chest with a slingshot—it's a must-see for any *Minecraft* or *Zelda* fan!

BIGGEST LET'S PLAYERS

IBALLISTICSQUID
NAME: DAVID SPENCER
- NO. OF FOLLOWERS: 3,300,000
- NO. OF VIEWS: 1,750,000,000

ABOUT: iBallisticSquid hails from Yorkshire in the UK. He's worked with loads of our favorite *Minecraft* Let's Players, including Stampy (who's also featured on this very page) and AmyLee33. If you're very smart, you might have noticed that David's PC *Minecraft* user name says iBalliisticSquid, rather than iBallisticSquid. No, it's not a typo—it's just that his preferred name was already taken when he signed up for the game!

GAME KNOWLEDGE	
FRIENDLINESS	
SKILL	4
ANGER	4
CRAFTING SKILLS	2
	4

VIKKSTAR123
NAME: VIKRAM BARN
- NO. OF FOLLOWERS: 2,900,000 ● NO. OF VIEWS: 583,000,000

ABOUT: Vik was born in Sheffield, UK, in 1995. His dedicated *Minecraft* channel features new videos daily, usually featuring his friends The Pack. Today, Vik lives with his friends who make up the Ultimate Sidemen team and yes, they also make videos for YouTube! He got amazing grades at the same time as running his very successful YouTube channels!

GAME KNOWLEDGE	
FRIENDLINESS	
SKILL	
ANGER	
CRAFTING SKILLS	2

INTHELITTLEWOOD
NAME: MARTYN LITTLEWOOD
- NO. OF FOLLOWERS: 1,300,000 ● NO. OF VIEWS: 260,000,000

ABOUT: Martyn Littlewood shot to YouTube fame by making video game parodies of famous songs, including *Form This Way*, a *Minecraft* parody of Lady Gaga's *Born This Way*. Martyn joined content creation team Yogcast in 2013 and has done tons of collaboration videos, including *Minecraft* vids with Stampy. He currently lives in Bristol, UK, with his cats.

GAME KNOWLEDGE	5
FRIENDLINESS	5
SKILL	4
ANGER	3
CRAFTING SKILLS	4

THEDIAMONDMINECART
NAME: DANIEL MIDDLETON
- NO. OF FOLLOWERS: 9,410,266 ● NO. OF VIEWS: 5,788,015,212

ABOUT: Daniel Middleton—also known as TheDiamondMinecart—has uploaded thousands of *Minecraft* videos since he started his YouTube channel in 2012. TheDiamondMinecart still posts *Minecraft* videos every day and also creates his own mods. Dan also holds a *Rocket League* record for scoring the most goals on 2v2 rookie mode!

GAME KNOWLEDGE	
FRIENDLINESS	4
SKILL	4
ANGER	3
CRAFTING SKILLS	

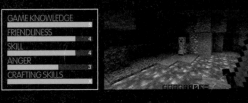

STAMPY
NAME: JOSEPH GARRETT
- NO. OF FOLLOWERS: 7,200,000 ● NO. OF VIEWS: 4,800,000,000

ABOUT: Stampy, aka Joseph Garrett, is an avid gamer hailing from the UK. He used to make videos part-time, but his quick rise to fame convinced him to give up his job to concentrate on making YouTube his career. He releases at least one new *Minecraft* video every single day, and in 2014 he was one of the top ten most-watched YouTube channels!

GAME KNOWLEDGE	5
FRIENDLINESS	5
SKILL	4
ANGER	1
CRAFTING SKILLS	

THE BEST WORLDS MADE BY MINECRAFT PLAYERS
COOLEST MAPS & MODS

HUNGER GAMES MINECRAFT MOD

PLAYER NAME Vikkstar123HD
LEVEL CREATOR Unknown

You've seen *The Hunger Games,* right? Where a group of people are dropped under a dome and left to fight to the death? Well, this is the same thing—but in *Minecraft*! Who will survive to the end and be crowned victor? There's only one way to find out …

BEST MOMENT

Vikk manages to last and be one of the final four players … only to fall down some stairs at the end.

MINECRAFT PORTAL MOD

PLAYER NAME Stampy and iBallisticSquid
LEVEL CREATORS VelcocityCinema, TheShowOfJordan

Even though Stampy isn't a fan of stunt maps, when he found out that there was a new *Portal*-flavored map he couldn't wait to try it out with iBallisticSquid. Watch them explore a blocky Aperture world in search of cake ingredients …

BEST MOMENT

Watching Stampy try (and quite often fail) to get through the map's jump puzzles never fails to make us laugh … which is great, because we also get to hear Stampy's awesome laugh, too!

STREAMERS' TOP TIPS

GETTING STARTED? WATCH VIDEOS!

If you're new to *Minecraft,* get on YouTube. People who know how to play are the best teachers—get the basics and then start experimenting.

WHEN IT'S DARK, IT'S DANGEROUS!

Things can get scary when the Sun goes down in *Minecraft.* You need to make a bed to sleep, find some food, and make some tools to get crafting.

HEY! STOP STEALING MY STUFF!

If you need to keep people from rooting through your valuables chest, place ice beneath some soul sand and everything will be super-slowed down.

BIN IT!

If you place a cactus on any sandy area and pop a trapdoor on top of it, you can create your own indoor trash bin. However, it will instantly destroy everything … including you.

HEROBRINE'S MANSION

PLAYER NAME AmyLee33
LEVEL CREATOR Hypixel

This is a must for any fan of *Minecraft* and horror—Herobrine's Mansion offers a spooky setting to explore. There are six boss fights, all-new monsters, shops, potions and even four secret rooms. Just don't go alone!

BEST MOMENT
Definitely the Witch fight. Amy and her sister Salem have to bring their A-game to defeat the incredibly hard enemy … and it's not an easy feat. Potion time!

THE DROPPER

PLAYER NAME Yogscast's Lewis and Simon
LEVEL CREATOR Bigre

It might seem simple, but there's only one rule in The Dropper—survive the fall. Pull the switch and do your best not to plummet down to Earth, dodging the (many) obstacles in your way as you go. Think it sounds easy? Uh, it's really not as simple as it sounds—trust us.

BEST MOMENT
Lewis and Simon have talked a lot about how much they hate jumping puzzles … so The Dropper—a map created just to fall—should be perfect for them … right?! WRONG!

STAR WARS ADVENTURE MAP

PLAYER NAME Keralis
LEVEL CREATOR Hypixel

It doesn't get much cooler than a *Star Wars* custom map. This one—simply called Star Wars—requires you to save hostages and disable an AT-AT walker on Hoth. It was the very first map created by Hypixel (who also contributed to several of the other maps included in this list).

BEST MOMENT
Someone needs to tell Keralis what you're supposed to do when you rescue hostages … we're not sure that saving them and then attacking them was the right thing to do!

VIKKSTAR123

With over 2 million subscribers, 500+ million views and thousands of *Minecraft* episodes, Vikkstar123 is one of the UK's biggest Let's Players, posting awesome new videos every single day.

Can you remember the first time you played *Minecraft*?
My friend said, "Hey, come and check this out," but the way he described it probably wasn't the best. He said, "You build houses, and zombies attack you, and you plant flowers and stuff." I was like: "What on earth?!" I had no idea! So I hopped on and played with them, but it didn't really turn out to be me being taught the game—it was just them messing with me, to be honest!

What about the first time that you uploaded a video?
After that first time, I made a little video and posted it on my YouTube channel that was mainly just shooter videos, and said, "Hey, would you guys like to see more of this?" A lot of people back then were like NO! No WAY! That's partially because I had no idea what was going on and at that time, audiences were very segregated. So I forgot about *Minecraft* for a little while, but when I got bored of doing shooters every day, I thought, why not make a new YouTube channel? I got the same friend back and said, "We're playing it properly this time!" I really enjoyed it. It didn't get the greatest reception, but it was enough for me to say I'm going to carry on doing this.

Why do you think your videos have been so successful?
Consistency is definitely the key. I made sure that when I started making *Minecraft* videos and people were enjoying them, I knew I was going to continue making two to three videos every single day, without fail. People who started watching my channel knew what to expect. Another thing I feel I've always done is improve my skills and try to be the best I can. I'll look up a lot of things, such as how to build certain automated machines. I'll look up mechanics and how things work, like the enchanted armor. I really made an effort to fully understand the game to the point that I could teach people things.

Why do you still play it?
I'm still learning to this day! It's crazy. Three years down the line, there's still new content to learn about, to understand. I still have fun playing it, and enjoying playing it with a lot of different friends.

TOP 10 FUNNIEST MINECRAFT HEROES

If variety is the spice of life, then these *Minecraft* heroes must be the spiciest gamers out there! Whether it's imaginary characters, hilarious fails, or ideas that even the craziest mind wouldn't (and shouldn't!) dream of, these personalities know how to entertain you with their hilarious acts.

1 STAMPY

The soothing voice of Stampy is always the sign of a good time, and we're amazed he can somehow keep track of the many characters he comes up with for his *Minecraft* stories! Energetic, lively, and fun, Stampy will cheer you up no matter how tough your day has been.

2 DANTDM

His mind races at a million miles an hour, since Dan's curiosity when playing *Minecraft* often overtakes the need for caution or care ... cue hilarity as he tumbles from one mishap to another, cracking jokes as he goes, and making himself laugh as much as he does his viewers.

3 LITTLELIZARDGAMING

If you want to take your foot off the gas when watching *Minecraft* videos, tune in to LittleLizard's YouTube channel. *Minecraft* school has lots of great advice and clever tips, but it's not all serious; LittleLizard also roleplays crazy scenarios to make sure you laugh as well as learn.

(4)

ETHOSLAB

If there is ever an award made for "Keeper of *Minecraft* Knowledge," then EthosLab deserves that crown immediately. He does things with *Minecraft* you wouldn't have thought possible, and his subtle, wry humor is a refreshing change from the other manic YouTube personalities.

(5) ### SKYDOESMINECRAFT

The beauty of SkyDoesMinecraft's channel is its simplicity. It's just him playing *Minecraft* with his friends and having a great time. You know how funny it is when your friends mess up? That is what SkyDoesMinecraft is all about.

JEROMEASF

It's not just plain old vanilla *Minecraft* that YouTubers are interested in. JeromeASF hunts down the strangest *Minecraft* mods, and his surprise at playing *Minecraft* block races or pirate island battles are what makes him so entertaining.

(6)

(7)

IBALLISTICSQUID

We imagine that the only time iBallisticSquid keeps quiet is when he goes to sleep! This YouTuber is simply bursting with energy—cracking jokes, chatting away—he could have a blank screen in *Minecraft* and still find a way to entertain you.

YOGSCAST LEWIS & SIMON

While Yogscast aren't *Minecraft* specialists, it's always great news when these sparkling personalities turn their attention to Mojang's blocky game. Check out their "Whale Lords" survival series for example, where they fly through the sky on the back of a giant whale.

(8)

(9)

BAJANCANADIAN

Watching BajanCanadian is a rollercoaster ride where you can't always see where the track is going. One second he's performing roleplay as a baby riding a magic pig, the next he's getting his fans involved as he challenges them at minigames!

(10) ### CAPTAINSPARKLEZ

Many have tried to copy his style, but no one comes close to CaptainSparklez and his stunning versatility. Watch his *Gangnam Style* parody in *Minecraft* and give it a try yourself— if you can capture even a tenth of his charisma and hilarity, we applaud you.

GET CREATIVE WITH MINECRAFT

THERE'S MORE TO DO THAN BUILDING!

ROLE-PLAYING

● *Minecraft* has always been a game that's about discovery, exploring, and making your own fun. That means it has never had a traditional story … but that's not to stop you from creating your own stories. That's exactly what the more creative minds on YouTube have been doing, as they fill Mojang's world with their own adventures and fantasy. Take SGCBarbierian for example: he makes things like his Minecraft City videos about moving into a huge town. It's far better than it sounds and a perfect example of how *Minecraft* has no limits when it comes to your imagination.

BUILD BATTLE

● One *Minecraft* trend you might not have heard of yet is Build Battle, a favorite of popular *Minecraft* YouTuber AmyLee33. The idea is that you and the other Build Battle competitors are given something to build in a small plot of land—a mouse, an igloo, Santa, or any other random thing you can think of—and have five minutes to build it. When time's up, you vote for each other's creations and the one with the most votes win. Sound good? You have no idea how fiercely competitive building a mouse can be, and the joy of emerging victorious is immense!

MAKING MINI GAMES

● If you don't like the games being made by other people in *Minecraft*, why not just make your own? You might be surprised to find that making them can be every bit as fun as playing them. Whether you follow iBallisticSquid's lead and make a racecourse, or are inspired by Longbow's "Giant Small" time trial filled with puzzles and platforming sections, there are lots of possibilities for making your own fun.

MODDING

● There are a bunch of *Minecraft* mods that change the way the game plays, to the point where you almost don't recognize that it's still *Minecraft*! Take the Pixelmon mod, for example, which turns *Minecraft* into *Pokémon*. Check out the likes of Stampy, iBallisticSquid, and Amy Lee33 playing the Pixelmon mod and catching blocky Pokémon on their channels.

SONG PARODIES

● If you're a fan of *Minecraft* and you love music, then you've got to check out Phantaboulous's YouTube channel. This creative mind takes pop songs you know and love like "All About That Bass" and "Birthday" but twists the lyrics to reflect *Minecraft* mishaps, like running away from Creepers. He even has unique *Minecraft* music videos to go with his parodies that will have you rolling around with laughter.

MAKE IT REAL

● The fun doesn't just begin and end on *Minecraft*'s servers, as the creativity it inspires spills out into the real world too. Not surprisingly, given the baking pun in her name, iHasCupquake bakes video-game-inspired treats, which include *Minecraft* cookies, a Creeper cake, and more.

DID YOU KNOW?

It's possible to make your own custom *Minecraft* skin and transport it into the game so you can play as that character.

THEMED WORLDS

● You love *Minecraft* ... but you might also love *Doctor Who*. Or *Skyrim*. Or steampunk. Themed packs let you combine your various loves with *Minecraft*, so you can start building that *Doctor Who* world you've always dreamt of. If you want to see good examples of this in action, watch Stampy and iBallisticSquid's themed world videos.

FUN YOUTUBE GAMES

YOUTUBE ISN'T JUST ABOUT MINECRAFT—THERE ARE LOTS OF FUN AND EXCITING GAMES ENJOYED BY YOUTUBE HEROES LIKE STAMPY AND DANTDM. HERE'S A LIST OF OUR FAVORITES!

▶ KING'S QUEST

PLAYED BY: **STAMPY, SOOO MUNGRY**

This medieval adventure game sees its hero, Graham, on a grand quest to become a knight. Old Graham narrates the story to his granddaughter Gwendolyn, and the decisions you make as young Graham change the narrative. It's interesting to see Stampy wrestle with some of the trickier decisions he has to make in *King's Quest*, along with some of the more challenging puzzles offered. Don't watch Stampy's playthrough until you've played it yourself and see how your decisions differ from his.

▶ ROBLOX

PLAYED BY: **AMYLEE33, DANTDM**

"I'm by the tin of beans" isn't something you normally hear players shout while playing games, but then again, *Roblox* is anything but normal. This creative PC game lets players build their own worlds using blocks and share those worlds with others, which means *Roblox* has everything from simple hide-and-seek challenges to tricky obstacle courses. Like *Minecraft*, it's just as much fun playing what creations others put together as it is creating levels yourself.

▶ RATCHET & CLANK

Galactic Range
Fairground

Step into the training course, and let's test your mettle.

PLAYED BY: STAMPY, THERADBRAD

The *Ratchet & Clank* series is known for having some of the coolest weaponry in gaming, and the latest outing on PS4 might be the coolest yet. The Glove of Doom throws out little robots that home in on any threats, the Groovitron disco ball causes bouts of uncontrollable dancing, and the Sheepinator turns enemies into explosive sheep. Even if you're not playing it yourself, the sci-fi weapons and gorgeous graphics make *Ratchet & Clank* a stunning game to watch.

▶ PLANTS VS. ZOMBIES: GARDEN WARFARE 2

PLAYED BY: STAMPY, ZACKSCOTTGAMES

Time-traveling bounty hunter oranges vs. zombie superheroes? Unicorn chompers that can burrow into the ground vs. hovering, spinning imps with rockets? The battles in *Plants vs. Zombies: Garden Warfare 2* are like nothing else in gaming, and seeing the weird and wonderful matchups play out, with the unique weapons for each character fizzing and popping, is what makes this game such a spectacle.

▶ SKYLANDERS SUPERCHARGERS

DIVE-CLOPS
1267

PLAYED BY: STAMPY, ETHANGAMERTV

It's one of the biggest games around so it's little wonder YouTubers have been giving *Skylanders* a try. What's interesting for *Skylanders* fans is watching the likes of Stampy and EthanGamerTV playing *SuperChargers* as characters and vehicles you might not have yourself, which could help you decide which character to choose next. Plus Stampy and Ethan are such great company, you'll happily watch them play as different *Skylanders* characters anyway!

▶ SLITHER.IO

PLAYED BY: LAURENZSIDE, GIZZY GAZZA

It might not look like much, but underneath its simple surface is a fierce snake vs. snake vs. snake multiplayer battle that's drawing more fans by the day. All you have to do is avoid crashing into the body of another player's snake … but that also means any other snake touching your body gets eliminated. Trying to twist your way around other players to set inescapable traps is fun, but nothing compares to the satisfying feeling of slithering away from another player trying to box you in.

▶ HAPPY WHEELS

PLAYED BY: **DANTDM, JACKSEPTICEYE**

Want to know why physics is cool? Because physics is what powers the fun in *Happy Wheels,* and it's hard to think of many games that will make you collapse with laughter like this can. Often the object is simply getting to the end of the obstacle course, but the exaggerated physics is your biggest enemy rather than the obstacles themselves, since anything less than the most precise controls results in hilarious crashes.

▶ ORI AND THE BLIND FOREST

PLAYED BY: **JACKSEPTICEYE, PYROPUNCHER**

This platformer is beautiful, unique, charming … and surprisingly difficult. You'll come for the lush graphics but you'll stay for the challenge. Watching skilled experts dance through the obstacles is mesmerizing, but it's just as much fun watching players try and figure out how to get through the intricate levels unscathed. You may even pick up a hint or two to help you progress in your own game.

▶ GOAT SIMULATOR

PLAYED BY: **EVANTUBEGAMING, DANTDM**

Rocket-powered goats, explosive gas stations, rollercoasters, and the longest tongue you've ever seen—it's little wonder YouTubers have flocked to the crazy world of *Goat Simulator.* Even though the maps are small, there's a dizzying amount of mayhem that can be caused, and that's what makes it such fun to watch *Goat Simulator* in action. You can't predict what will happen next … the only certainty is that it will make you howl with laughter.

▶ KERBAL SPACE PROGRAM

PLAYED BY: **SCOTT MANLEY, FAR LANDS OR BUST**

This fantastic combination of science and gaming is at its best when things go wrong. The slightest miscalculation means air-bound contraptions go flying, which means a trip back to the drawing board and trying to figure out where the rockets should be, at what angle, and how hard they should be firing. It's a fascinating game to watch, since everyone has different ideas … Scott Manley does a great job of breaking down the science behind the game. Make sure you watch his informative videos!

► LEGO JURASSIC WORLD

PLAYED BY: **EVANTUBEGAMING**

The LEGO spin on the big-screen series is fun, not just because of the blocky interpretation of famous scenes from the movies, but also because of the smashing and building that takes place in every game. LEGO bricks exploding everywhere is a sight to see, but it's even more fun to watch as multiple players try and coordinate the chaos, working together to crack the complicated puzzles. If you can tear yourself away from playing *LEGO Jurassic Worlds*, it's worth watching the videos from EvanTubeGaming—they're a lot of fun.

► THE ESCAPISTS

PLAYED BY: **DANTDM, IHASCUPQUAKE**

All you have to do in this cutesy game featuring adorable pixel characters is escape … but as you can imagine, this is a difficult task. There are plenty of different ways to escape, and watching YouTubers try to figure out how to scramble to freedom is weirdly engaging. Can DanTDM figure out how papier maché, soap, and wire leads to freedom? Will iHasCupquake work out the prisoner routine and use it to her advantage?

► WORMS BATTLEGROUNDS

PLAYED BY: **XCAGE**

The *Worms* series is famous for its multiplayer battles, pitching two teams of worms against each other as they use highly powered weapons to chip away at the other team's health bars … including weapons such as explosive sheep! The mix of strategy and mayhem is what has made the *Worms* series so popular—and has done for so many years now—and *Worms Battlegrounds* cranks up the chaos, making it a great YouTube watch.

► SKATE 3

PLAYED BY: **ZEXYZEK, DANTDM**

Disaster awaits you in *Skate 3*, a game where more fun is had crashing into obstacles than in successfully grinding rails or powersliding around corners. It's the physics of each crash that makes this so fun to watch, the skateboarder flopping around like a boneless chicken after each crash. That's why so many YouTubers have flocked to play it and why it has been such a popular game for others to watch.

THE LITTLE GAME THAT COULD

STARDEW VALLEY

One ~~me~~ *eally old piece of pottery. It had* ~~writi~~ *on* ~~tha~~ *couldn't read.*

It's not always the biggest games that prove to be massive hits with the Twitch community. Every now and then, an indie hit bubbles up out of nowhere to prove surprisingly popular—*Don't Starve* and *I Am Bread* are two examples—but by far the biggest surprise success is *Stardew Valley*. A simple farming game at its heart, inspired by the classic *Harvest Moon* series,

the livestreaming community has come together to see who can pry the hidden secrets from this wonderful game first. It's even managed to pull in more daily viewers on Twitch than *Minecraft*, *World of Tanks*, *Super Mario Maker,* and *World of Warcraft*, proving that sometimes the little games do have what it takes to compete with the gigantic triple-A blockbusters!

DID YOU KNOW?

Stardew Valley was created by one developer, Eric Barone, who spent 70 hours a week for four years making it.

TOP 3 STREAM MOMENTS

THE HYPE TRAIN BUILDS
SEPTEMBER 23, 2015

1 Only the most dedicated fans of indie gaming had even heard of *Stardew Valley* … until this stream by the game's publisher, Chucklefish. Word went around forums and social media about this fascinating new game, and soon, thousands and thousands of curious gamers were watching the stream. This was the moment that *Stardew Valley* became *the* game to watch!

STARDEW VALLEY IS RELEASED
FEBRUARY 26, 2016

2 With sole developer Eric Barone keeping fans up to date with all the happenings ahead of release date, the day *Stardew Valley* was finally open to all was a huge moment on Twitch. Streamers immediately jumped on the farming sim and starting casting it to thousands and thousands of viewers.

THE LONE DEVELOPER GETS STUCK IN
MARCH 13, 2016

3 Even though *Stardew Valley* has been released to fantastic sales and critical acclaim, single developer Eric Barone knows his work isn't done. He releases frequent updates that add new content, and in March 2016, he told fans about the biggest one yet, adding dialogue for couples who are married in the game.

BIGGEST STREAMERS

COHHCARNAGE

NAME: BEN
- NO. OF FOLLOWERS: 555,000
- NO. OF VIEWS: 29,000,000

ABOUT: CohhCarnage is known for getting involved with lots of different games, so it's no surprise *Stardew Valley* eventually caught his attention. He likes to play one game at a time, uploading multiple episodes before moving on to his next challenge. He keeps up a constant dialogue with his viewers while playing, making his streams interesting and engaging at all times. So, for great game tips with enthusiastic commentary, CohhCarnage is definitely worth checking out.

HILARIOUSNESS	2
TALKATIVENESS	3
ANGER	2
KNOWLEDGE	4
SKILL	2

JONBAMS

NAME: JON BAMS
- NO. OF FOLLOWERS: 190,000
- NO. OF VIEWS: 7,200,000

ABOUT: Is there anyone with a better voice online? JonBams has a voice that's made for radio, and he talks without rambling. Combine this silky-smooth voice with the chilled-out nature of *Stardew Valley* and you'll soon see all of your stress and troubles just melt away. Who knew watching someone tend to virtual vegetables could be so enjoyable?

HILARIOUSNESS	4
TALKATIVENESS	4
ANGER	2
KNOWLEDGE	3
SKILL	2

ARTEMIS

NAME: SARAH
- NO. OF FOLLOWERS: 94,000
- NO. OF VIEWS: 1,100,000

ABOUT: While the calm nature of *Stardew Valley* tends to have a relaxing effect on those playing it, Australian streamer Artemis manages to keep her enthusiastic streaming style going. Always chatting to her viewers and with her own music playing in the background, it's an interesting contrast to the game's laid-back nature.

HILARIOUSNESS	2
TALKATIVENESS	5
ANGER	3
KNOWLEDGE	2
SKILL	3

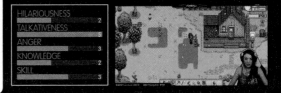

SOARYN

NAME: UNKNOWN
- NO. OF FOLLOWERS: 120,000
- NO. OF VIEWS: 3,400,000

ABOUT: One of the fastest talkers on Twitch, even *Stardew Valley* has a somewhat relaxing effect on Soaryn … but he still has a lot to say! Soaryn is known for his *Minecraft* streams, but like many other big streamers, even he couldn't resist the lure of *Stardew Valley* and had to discover its hidden secrets.

HILARIOUSNESS	2
TALKATIVENESS	5
ANGER	2
KNOWLEDGE	4
SKILL	4

LOSERFRUIT

NAME: KATHLEEN
- NO. OF FOLLOWERS: 180,000
- NO. OF VIEWS: 4,600,000

ABOUT: Laid-back Australian LoserFruit is excellent company if you want to chill out. Her fun demeanor combined with the slow, gentle pace of *Stardew Valley*, makes for one of the most relaxing experiences you can have watching streams. If you want to get away from the site's manic screaming, find LoserFruit, kick off your shoes, and relax a little.

HILARIOUSNESS	2
TALKATIVENESS	3
ANGER	1
KNOWLEDGE	3
SKILL	3

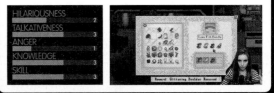

GET SOME

DOTA 2

Since its release back in July 2013, *Dota 2* has become a phenomenon, selling millions of copies and averaging an incredible 600,000 players every single month. Its fast-paced, tactical gameplay has also made it one of the most exciting eSports to watch, as teams who specialize in Multiplayer Online Battle Arena games fight it out in huge competitions.

The game is all about teamwork, with heroes dividing across the map to attack and defend against the opposition team through "lanes" that join two bases. Unlike *League of Legends* and other MOBAs, there's a much harsher punishment for dying in *Dota 2*, which makes it much harder to learn. However, this makes competition between top players even fiercer!

DID YOU KNOW?

If you look closely, the Treant Protector hero (who is a tree) has "Riki was 'ere" etched into its side by the sneaky hero Riki!

TOP 3 STREAMS

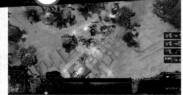

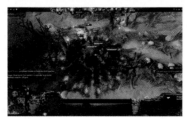

GANGNAM STYLE!
AUGUST 8, 2013

1 When Danil "Dendi" Ishutin was competing with team Natus Vincere at The International 2013 (a major eSports tournament), he used a brilliant play to capture and kill a member of the opposition team. After the move, he ran from his team's booth on stage and celebrated by doing a Gangnam Style dance in front of the crowd!

THE PLAY
SEPTEMBER 1, 2015

2 Natus Vincere vs. Invictus Gaming at The International 2015 will go down in history for a moment of near perfection. "The Play," as it was later named, saw NaVi's Enigma lock down the attacking IG players, then a NaVi Juggernaut spins his blades on the trapped IG team, resulting in instant death for the team.

PARENTS CAN BE EMBARRASSING ONLINE!
JUNE 30, 2015

3 This was a lesson Arteezy learned while he was loading up a match. While streaming, his dad decided to walk in and proceeded to flick him on the ear. Hilarity ensued, along with multiple uploads of the incident on YouTube. Parents!

STREAMERS' TOP CHARACTER PICKS

RAIJIN THUNDERKEG

PLAYER NAME: SUMAIL
PRIMARY ROLE: Initiator, Nuker, Carry, Disabler, Escape

STATS

INTELLIGENCE	23+2.6
DAMAGE	22-32
AGILITY	22+1.8
MOVESPEED	285
STRENGTH	19+1.5
ARMOR	2

Wielding the elemental power of lightning, Raijin Thunderkeg has strong mobility and is a good carrier. Static Remnant lets the Storm Spirit create a clone of himself capable of shocking enemies within the area, and on top of that, it has a super-short cooldown. Combine that with his Ultimate ability, Ball Lightning, and you're good to go.

ABILITIES

Static Remnant

Electric Vortex

Overload

Ball Lightning

SHENDELZARE

PLAYER NAME: PURGEGAMERS
PRIMARY ROLE: Nuker, Support, Disabler, Escape

STATS

INTELLIGENCE	15+1.75
DAMAGE	12-26
AGILITY	27+3.3
MOVESPEED	300
STRENGTH	18+2.6
ARMOR	0

Shendelzare the Vengeful Spirit is where it's at if you want to gank, disable, or strengthen your team. Her Support skill set makes it easy to set up kills for her team, Magic Missile offers up a decent stun move, and an armor reduction debuff in Wave of Terror is always handy.

ABILITIES

Magic Missile

Wave of Terror

Vengeance Aura

Nether Swap

IO

PLAYER NAME: BIG DADDY/NOTAIL
PRIMARY ROLE: Nuker, Support, Escape

STATS

INTELLIGENCE	23+1.7
DAMAGE	26-35
AGILITY	14+1.6
MOVESPEED	295
STRENGTH	17+1.9
ARMOR	2

Io the Guardian Wisp has a lot of options, from materializing an ally anywhere on the map to harassing enemies out of their lane with the Spirits ability. Also, unlike other heroes, this little wisp doesn't need to face enemies to attack, so you can keep hitting while you run.

ABILITIES

Tether

Break Tether

Spirits

Overcharge

Relocate

PRO INTERVIEW

TAMMY "FURRYFISH" TANG

Tammy Tang has held the all-girl team Asterisk* together for over 10 years. Not only is she a highly skilled *Dota 2* player, she's also a coach, a captain, an administrative assistant, and a CEO all rolled into one.

How did you get into competitive *Dota*?

I was playing *Counter-Strike* competitively in a female team—from around 1998 till 2002—so the idea of playing a computer game competitively was not new to me. After my A-levels (the equivalent of completing high school in the United States), I started playing the newest game on the market, which was *WarCraft III*, and I played many custom games. *Dota* was one of those.

What is an average day for you like in terms of training?

At our peak, we were playing together online daily, for at least five games a night, and I was doing 13 to 15 games a day. We also met up twice a week at LAN to play together in real life. Our own lives mostly took second place—our schedules revolved around training—meaning we requested for family dinners or Valentine's day dates to fit our training schedules, and not the other way around!

What strengths do you bring to the Asterisk* roster?

On my mixed team, I was the captain and drafter and I called all the shots, so I brought that to Asterisk*. Sometimes, you don't have to make a perfect call, you just need to make a call—someone needs to make a call—so that you give people direction and focus.

If you could give any advice to prospective competitive players, what would it be?

Do not be deluded. You have to be very clear on how good you are. Don't try to cheat yourself into thinking you're world class when you're just not there. There are two ways to get there—either to have an immense amount of innate talent, or to work exceptionally hard (and work with a focus, not aimlessly).

PLAY YOUR CARDS RIGHT

HEARTHSTONE: HEROES OF WARCRAFT

What do 40 million players and 220,000 YouTube subscribers have in common? They're all obsessed with one of the most watched and played online collectible card games: *Hearthstone*. This free-to-play fantasy game made by notorious developer Blizzard was the fourth most-watched on Twitch in 2015, with almost 400 million hours watched by fans—

which is no mean feat considering it was only released in 2014. Being able to play *Hearthstone* on a PC, Mac, iOS, or Android device has enabled more and more people to start dealing out cards wherever they might be. So you can master these tips from the top players and streamers in the world sitting in your bedroom, traveling on the bus, or even sunbathing on a beach!

DID YOU KNOW? The Innkeeper's Journal blog from Blizzard is worth keeping an eye on. Posts have revealed new cards!

TOP **3** STREAM MOMENTS

LONGEST TURN EVER
MARCH 25, 2015

1 Mamytwink set a new record when he made a turn last 45 hours and 18 minutes—that's almost two days! Thanks to nine Arcane Missile cards and 206 copies of Velen's Chosen, Mamytwink could then use cloned copies of Prophet Velen to multiply the total spell damage.

KRIPPARRIAN'S CLUTCH WIN
JUNE 19, 2015

2 After a series of short, 15-second turns left his defenses crippled, Kripparrian was ready to give up on this match. But he got incredibly lucky by getting the Sacrificial Pact card, which instantly killed the enemy and won him the game when he was seconds away from losing.

BOOM TOWN
MAY 14, 2015

3 With only seven health points, the only solution for Amaz was to pray that his two Boom Bot cards would deal damage to the enemy's. They did and were destroyed in the process, with the resulting explosion killing the enemy summoner and winning the game!

BIGGEST STREAMERS

NL_KRIPP
NAME: OCTAVIAN MOROSAN
● NO. OF FOLLOWERS: **750,000** ● NO. OF VIEWS: **128,500,000**

ABOUT: Being voted "Favourite Hearthstone Stream" is no surprise, since Kripparrian has been a seasoned streamer and YouTuber for years—he previously filmed popular *World of Warcraft* tutorials. In addition to his streams, Kripp also produces multiple videos every day for his YouTube channel and occasionally casts events, including the 2015 World Championships.

HILARIOUSNESS	4
ENTHUSIASM	4
ANGER	4
KNOWLEDGE	4
TALKATIVENESS	5

Jaina Proudmoore
30

ITSHAFU
NAME: RUMAY WANG
● NO. OF FOLLOWERS: **405,000** ● NO. OF VIEWS: **45,500,000**

ABOUT: Previously a *World of Warcraft* pro, Hafu is one of the top female *Hearthstone* streamers. While she is considered quieter than some of the other streamers, Hafu is one of the most watched players since she often collaborates with other top streamers. Hafu is also known for her arena plays and strategy discussion.

HILARIOUSNESS	3
ENTHUSIASM	4
ANGER	3
KNOWLEDGE	4
TALKATIVENESS	4

AMAZHS
NAME: JASON CHAN
● NO. OF FOLLOWERS: **685,000** ● NO. OF VIEWS: **53,000,000**

ABOUT: Team Archon's creator AmazHS was also the first-ever member of Liquid's *Hearthstone* team. AmazHS was a fan of other Blizzard games *Warcraft III* and *World of Warcraft* before becoming instantly hooked on *Hearthstone*. He's won big tournaments like IEM Shenzhen, and he casted the *Hearthstone* World Championships in 2015.

HILARIOUSNESS	3
ENTHUSIASM	4
ANGER	3
KNOWLEDGE	5
TALKATIVENESS	4

FORSENLOL
NAME: SEBASTIAN FORS
● NO. OF FOLLOWERS: **480,000** ● NO. OF VIEWS: **35,000,000**

ABOUT: Forsenlol was a professional *Starcraft* player before getting into *Hearthstone*, and he regularly enjoys taking part in invitational matches. After constructing his famous Miracle Rogue deck, Forsenlol built a very loyal fanbase on Twitch. It's all thanks to being an entertaining streamer and enabling a very active chat.

HILARIOUSNESS	4
ENTHUSIASM	3
ANGER	4
KNOWLEDGE	3
TALKATIVENESS	4

REYNAD27
NAME: ANDREY YANYUK
● NO. OF FOLLOWERS: **420,000** ● NO. OF VIEWS: **28,000,000**

ABOUT: The owner of Team Archon is no stranger to streaming and competitive tournaments himself, and his previous experience in trading card games like *Magic: The Gathering* enabled him to become both a notable player and streamer. While known for being "salty," or agitated, on stream, Reynad is also one of the most hardworking personalities.

HILARIOUSNESS	4
ENTHUSIASM	4
ANGER	3
KNOWLEDGE	5
TALKATIVENESS	4

UNIQUE DECKS & POWERFUL
CARDS USED BY THE PROS

STREAMERS' TOP PICKS

Thrall 30

Uther Lightbringer 30

WARRIOR

2

STREAMER: MaSsanSC
DECK TYPE: Control

A control Warrior deck's main goal is to force your opponent into a corner, improving your defenses and cleaning the board should there be any threats. Keep constant pressure with deathrattle cards and ensure your enemy can't play any large mana cards even in the late game.

WHY THEM?
To establish early control, use Revenge to clear the board. It'll pave the way for more annoying cards.

Revenge

Deal 1 damage to all minions. If you have 12 or less Health, deal 3 damage instead.

DRAGON PRIEST

2

STREAMER: Reynad
DECK TYPE: Control

The right wombo combo of dragon synergies can unleash some scary beasts. The Battlecry of Wyrmrest Agent, for example, provides a dragon card with a taunt, and the Priest Hero Power can keep healing the dragons. Reynad's variant of this deck provides a better "early curve," which means the deck is stronger at the start of the match.

WHY THEM?
Shrinkmeister is pretty versatile—great at keeping your early game in control and boosting your dragons, while you can also combine it with the Shadow Word cards, for example.

Shrinkmeister

Battlecry: Give a minion -2 Attack this turn.

3 **2**

STREAMERS' TOP TIPS

BEGINNER

EARLY GAME

MID-MATCH

ADVANCED

YOU DON'T HAVE TO PAY TO PLAY
When you first start playing *Hearthstone*, there are lots of cards to buy with "Dust." But you don't have to spend anything to make a deck!

BUILD YOUR DECK
Making your first deck will be tough, but you can upgrade it every time you open a new Expert pack to make it stronger. Don't worry, deck building is a difficult skill that takes time to master.

DON'T RUSH THE COIN
Okay so it's all shiny and gold, but dropping the Coin card in the first turn is a bit of a waste. Save it for later—use it to fill in gaps in future turns or use it in a combo to clear the board.

ARCANE DUST
Only Disenchant what you don't need, and don't be put off by those Legendaries just because they cost 1,600 dust each. Ragnaros the Firelord is a great, versatile card for most decks.

FREEZE MAGE

STREAMER: Kolento
DECK TYPE: Combo

Staying alive to draw out the perfect card mix can be boring, but once you get Alexstrasza plus a bunch of burn spells like Fireball and Forgotten Torch to reduce HP, you can easily one-turn kill your opponent. It's an exciting and satisfying combo.

WHY THEM?

Released with the League of Explorers expansion, Forgotten Torch is a cheaper alternative to Fireball. It costs one mana crystal less, but rains the same amount of damage as the four-mana Fireball.

3

Forgotten Torch

Deal 3 damage. Shuffle a 'Roaring Torch' into your deck that deals 6 damage.

3

Shade of Naxxramas

Stealth: At the start of your turn, gain +1/+1.

2 **2**

SECRET PALADIN

STREAMER: StrifeCro
DECK TYPE: Midrange

Early board control is key to this Secret Paladin deck. Mysterious Challenger is crucial in the sixth turn, as the instant multiple Secrets that are fished out of the deck can tremble most opponents. Add Lay on Hands for more flexibility and longevity, and you've got yourself a competitive deck.

WHY THEM?

As one of the Secret cards that are essential to Secret Paladin, vengeance is even more sweet when you use Avenge, with a +3/+2 boost in attempts to immortalize your hand.

AMNESIA YETI DRUID

STREAMER: AmazHS **DECK TYPE:** Combo

This Druid deck revolves around getting useful early cards like Darnassus and Innervate out for extra mana crystals. This will mean that you should be able to place a four-mana Savage Combatant out on the third turn, which is really fast, and then prepare for the all-important combos with draw cards.

WHY THEM?

Shade of Naxxramas allows a lot of sneaky, constant stat building. If your opponent lets it mount up before it finally comes out of Stealth, it'll be sure to give them a scare.

1

Avenge

Secret: When one of your minions dies, give a random friendly minion +3/+2.

FIREBAT

He was the winner of the Hearthstone World Championships in 2014, and he's the top-earning *Hearthstone* player of all time. But Firebat is more than just a prizewinning competitor, he's an avid community teacher too . . . .

How did you get into the scene?
I got into the competitive scene by qualifying for and ultimately winning the World Championship. Up until the point where my ladder performance enabled me to play in New York, I really didn't even have many of the cards and played the game because I enjoyed it, not because I thought I could make money or anything like that.

You've won $215,000 in your career—the highest amount a player has earned in *Hearthstone*—what sets you apart from other players?
I feel like my main difference was that I wanted it more than other people. I've always been out of place in school, or at work, but playing games really is my escape, and winning even more so. I spent over two months making spreadsheets and playing thousands of games before the World Championship, and I felt that I should put two years' worth of work into this one tournament because if I win, I will earn two-years' worth of my normal salary. There are photos that the casters took of the World Championship practice area, and I was literally the only one there most of the time. People really pass *Hearthstone* off as all randomness, but I truly believe hard work pays off in the end.

How do you keep on top of your game?
I play and talk with other players. I really value others' opinions and play practice games against people of all levels. I think that getting second opinions and thoughts can really help jump-start ideas and break boundaries with deck building.

You were the 2014 World Champion—but unfortunately you did not qualify for BlizzCon in 2015. Is there anything that you would have done differently?
Although I didn't qualify for BlizzCon, I was still able to be the highest prize winner, so I feel my strategies were sound. I do think for BlizzCon I played it too safe and I am not as hungry for success as I once was due to the fact that I don't need to win to get by anymore. Before, if I lost—that was it: The dream would be done for me. Now I have too much breathing room and it takes away from what made me the strongest player in 2014.

STAT ATTACK

179,731 billion
shells fired by
March 2016

18,011
battles fought
per hour

WORLD OF TANKS

World of Tanks has been unstoppable since a humble Russian demo rumbled onto the battlefield back in 2009, with just six vehicles and one map. The number of vehicles and maps has skyrocketed since then, as has the number of players, and the tank warfare game has now been released on Xbox 360, Xbox One and PS4 alongside its original home on PC.

60,158
repair kits used per hour

72,769
total number of clans

ON THE UP
Since broadcasting her first livestream in August 2015, Suzy Lu has gained over 20,000 eager followers and earned a Twitch partnership.

A DAY IN THE LIFE OF ...

SUZY LU

AS ONE OF THE BEST NEW NAMES ON THE RISE, SCOTTISH STREAMER SUZY LU TAKES US BEHIND THE SCENES ON HER LIFE

A typical day varies due to working for so many different websites—YouTube, Twitch, and so on. I have been livestreaming since August 2015 and my numbers have grown very quickly, and continue to rise. There is a lot of work that goes into streaming but it's very rewarding, and to know you are creating such a positive community makes the long hours 100 percent worth it. Most streamers tend to focus on just the one streaming website—however, I also work with specific gaming companies and YouTube to cover the latest releases every month and attend events to talk to those who are just starting their journey into the gaming industry. Gaming has always been one of my biggest passions, and to get the chance to share it with so many amazing people makes me smile every day. You don't get much better than that!

8:00 a.m.

Every morning I'm awake around 8:00 a.m., not by choice, as I'm not a morning person at all! But my main focus is to check my emails and Twitter to see what games are trending or due out in the next few days. It's important to stay on top of the latest releases. I do my absolute best to respond to all my followers' tweets, but as we are growing that is becoming harder now. I find it easier to manage the streams and YouTube myself, so I don't partner up with side networks or hire anyone to manage my emails. That way I know what I am doing for the week and hopefully nothing can go wrong with the schedule. Most of my morning consists of me of drinking lots of tea and eating toast.

10:00 a.m.

After I have taken my lovely doggie out for a walk I set up all my equipment to record for YouTube. I tend to record different style games for YouTube than what I will play live on Twitch. The videos vary according to what is trending at the time or just what I think the subscribers would like to see, such as maybe an up-to-date vlog on my life or a fun little Star Wars video. For the channel, I find it easier to play small, fun games then a full Let's Play on stream.

WOOF WOOF!

Recording usually takes a couple of hours, then it's another two or so hours to edit and upload to YouTube. Recording is so much fun, and when you see it all come together, you just can't wait for your audience to watch it.

"I do my absolute best to respond to all my followers' tweets"

1:00 p.m.

It's not always in the afternoon that I sit down to practice my singing, but I am currently working on an album, and I find once I have done some YouTube recording that my voice is warmed up and it's a great time to practice.

SUZY LU

I recently started to sing a lot more on stream, and it's become quite a feature now with followers asking me to sing! I have been singing since I was very young and I'm very passionate about music, so to get this opportunity is amazing. This diary will make it seem like I never leave the house, but I promise I do.

4:30 p.m.

This is my favorite part of the day. An hour before we go live on Twitch, I am usually creating hype with followers on Twitter, getting everyone ready for the stream of the day. I stream every day and play a huge variety of games. There will always be something going wrong with my equipment before or during the stream but I just work through it and try to laugh it off with everyone. My favorite part of being a streamer is interacting with my audience, and even though we are getting bigger, I will still try my hardest to make everyone feel included. I remember having 2,000 viewers and still trying to chat to everyone, not the easiest task but it was great fun. Depending on how my day has gone, or what games I'm covering I may have to start streams a little later on, which works for the American audience.

9:00 p.m.

Our streams are usually really busy with a lot of people chatting, so it takes me most of the night to unwind. After a stream, I tend to upload highlights from the stream to Twitter and interact with the audience a little bit more off stream, to keep that personal touch with everyone. This is usually my time to continue editing YouTube videos, or I will go and see my friends for a little bit. Funnily enough, I usually finish a stream, go see my friends, and end

up back playing the PlayStation again anyway, just with them! My controller never seems to be out of my hands. This is the only time I get the chance to play games off-stream or not on YouTube, so it's nice to still have that time to not take it seriously and play badly.

11:00 p.m.

This is the best time of the night to chat with my American audience and also to keep in touch with gaming companies across the pond. I find, like most streamers, that I end up living by American time more than UK time, which is why we get such little sleep. Most of the time new games are released at midnight, and if I feel It's something the audience will love, I am more than happy to stay up and stream it throughout the night or create YouTube videos for it. Streaming can be pretty flexible, which is the beauty of it. You can fit it around most projects and it will always bring in new people from all over the world. The gaming industry has brought so many special people into my life, and I often wonder what I would be doing if I didn't start it back in August 2015. I'm always grateful for the support of the audience and for the opportunities given to me by the gaming companies.

Suzy Lu x

This is just one day in the life of a live streamer. Every streamer is different and has their own way of doing things. For me personally, I find streaming from the PlayStation 4 to be my main focus, but I am hoping to branch into Xbox One and PC in the near future, to widen the audience even more.

Streaming is not always easy, but it is fun and you never know what adventure it might take you on next. If you want to be a professional streamer, be ready for a lot of work, but also have fun with it. When I started it was just to create a fun loving community, but now it's like an extended family that I'm grateful for daily! Believe in yourself and you can do anything.

TOP 10 TIPS

TO GET STARTED ON TWITCH

REMEMBER!
You have to be over 13 to use YouTube and Twitch!

1 CREATE AN ACCOUNT

● Before you can do anything, you'll need a Twitch account. Simply head over to **twitch.tv** and click the Sign Up button on the top right. You'll need to choose a username that isn't already taken (keep trying names until you get a green check), and add a password that nobody else can guess.

2 CHOOSE YOUR GAME

● You have two options when it comes to streaming games on Twitch. You can either play a game that nobody else is streaming to try and start a new trend, or go for a game that's already huge on Twitch, like *League of Legends*, and compete with all the big names!

3 GET A WEBCAM

● You can stream without a webcam, but people are more likely to watch if they can see your face and your reactions to what's going on in your game. Get a good webcam and set it up—or use the Kinect or PlayStation Camera if you are streaming a console game.

4

USE A GOOD MIC
● Our best tip is not to use a poor-quality microphone. That means avoiding cheap chat headsets, and steering clear of using the built-in microphone on your computer. Get a good quality USB microphone if you can—crackly sound will only make viewers tune out!

5

GET THE APP
● If you're on Xbox One or PS4, download the Twitch app to your console and log into your account. From here you can set up streaming of your game fairly quickly. On PC or Mac, get hold of broadcasting software, such as OBS or Wirecraft, to get a ton of customization options to play around with.

6

MAKE A HUD
● If you want to look really professional, you can create an overlay, known as a HUD, that will sit over the top of the game you're playing and show things like your webcam image, text, and images. Take a look at how streamers do this to get ideas for how you want yours laid out, and remember to keep the onscreen gameplay free of clutter.

7

CUSTOMIZE YOUR PROFILE
● Make your profile interesting! Add a custom profile picture, create an image to display when you're offline, and add information to the info boxes that sit below your stream when people visit your page. These info boxes can be anything from an About Me section to a place to explain any chat rules that you may have.

8

DO MORE THAN PLAY
● Remember—you're not just playing a game on your own any more! You have to be entertaining to the people who are watching as well. Our best advice is to pretend there is someone in the room with you. Chat to them, explain what you're doing, and if someone asks you something in chat, answer them.

9

KEEP TO A SCHEDULE
● You can't expect people to just randomly tune in if you don't tell them when you'll be online! Create a schedule, so your fans know to come back every day or week to get their latest fix of streaming goodness. But be sensible and don't let streaming take over your life!

10

DON'T BE AFRAID TO BAN
● One thing you can expect to get a fair amount of in the Twitch chat is negative commenters. But don't worry—some viewers will just be offering constructive criticism to help you improve. If you aren't comfortable with someone's comments, though, don't be afraid to ban them!

HOW TO ...
GROW YOUR twitch AUDIENCE

YOU'VE GOT THE EQUIPMENT. YOU'VE GOT THE GAMES. YOU'VE STARTED STREAMING. BUT HOW DO YOU GET PEOPLE TO WATCH? HERE'S HOW TO TAKE YOUR FIRST STEPS TOWARDS GROWING AN AUDIENCE ...

Pro Clubs = w\viewers
102 viewers on XboxSector

Legend Four Grind!
76 viewers on goatgetsdubs

Road To Champ 1
52 viewers on Danoxide

!points | C.R.E.A.M| PvP Until appoi...
51 viewers on JarJarMerks

STREAM ON CONSOLE!

● Streaming on PC is super competitive, but the viewing numbers are way lower on PlayStation 4 and Xbox One. It's much easier to make it to the top of the pile, and cracking the top eight will even land you a spot on the front page of Twitch. There aren't too many prolific console streamers yet, so give it a try!

CREATE A SCHEDULE!

● One of the most important things you can do right from the start is create a schedule. This means viewers who want to see you in action again will know when you'll next be streaming and will likely make a note to tune in. Even better is if you can plan what games you'll be playing and make them part of your public schedule as well. Remember though—once you've created a schedule, stick to it! There's nothing worse than disappointing your Twitch fans.

WHY DO YOU WATCH TWITCH?

This is the first question you should ask yourself before deciding how to grow your Twitch channel! Think about why you watch Twitch streams and what it is that you like about watching, and then you can start honing your approach …

ARE YOU DRAWN TO PERSONALITIES?

● Of course you are—everyone is! You might think it's hard to force it on camera but that's only because people try to force a funny personality. Think about what people like about you and focus on that. It could be your dry humor, your enthusiastic nature, your warm personality, your ridiculous knowledge …

IS PEOPLE PLAYING UNUSUAL GAMES YOUR THING?

● You can dig into your own library of unusual and exciting games to offer something new and interesting to your Twitch audience! Games like pigeon-dating sim *Hatoful Boyfriend*, steampunk-puzzle *Ironcast*, or time-rewinding platformer *Replay: VHS Is Not Dead* are great examples of cool, unique games that fit in this category.

DO YOU LIKE WATCHING AMAZING GAMERS DOMINATING MULTIPLAYER?

● You can't just do this without practice, of course. It's not like you can waltz into a game of FIFA and start racking up the goals! But you might want to consider one of the games you're best at and sticking with it. Viewers will tune in to see your skills and you'll get to enjoy playing your favorite game to boot.

SPEAK OUT!

● Use a microphone to interact with your audience! Remember that the key to livestreaming is that it's about the viewers, not about you. Talk to them. Respond to any interesting comments in Twitch chat. React to funny things that happen within your game!

BE PATIENT!

Remember that it takes time to grow an audience! Create a schedule and stick to it. Find your speciality and stick to it. Keep streaming and stick to it! There's no magic wand you can wave for thousands of viewers to turn up overnight, so keep at it and be patient. If you enjoy streaming anyway, do it because you love it and reap the rewards later!

SHARE THE LOVE!

● There's a pretty good chance your regular viewers will be streamers as well. After all, most of them are already signed up to Twitch! When you're done streaming, make sure you send your viewers onto another stream, ideally one of the streams your viewers have started. This is known as a "raid," and that streamer will remember and is likely to return the favor.

TRY DUAL WIELDING!

● One good way to buddy up is to do "dual streams." This is when you play the game with another streamer, which can be cooperatively (teaming up on *League of Legends*, for example) or competitively (taking each other on in *League of Legends*!). This means fans of their channel will check out your stream as well!

LEAHLOVESCHIEF

TWITCH'S LIVELIEST STREAMER SPEAKS OUT!

Being a positive home for a lot of people is a nice feeling.

STARTING OUT

What was it that made you start streaming?

● When Xbox One came out I heard about their Twitch app that allowed you to stream straight from the Xbox and was instantly intrigued—I'd heard of Twitch Plays Pokémon, but the idea of playing video games with other people watching was weird but interesting.

I figured I talked to myself enough while I was gaming, so why not see if other people wanted to hear what I had to say as well? Turned out people did want to hear, and they enjoyed my reactions to the games I played.

What do you think helped your audience grow?

● Before I streamed I was—and still am!—a cosplayer and that's what gave me a little start. I had just finished a *Destiny* cosplay and *Destiny* was the main game I was streaming. On my fifth or so stream I cosplayed in my *Destiny* cosplay and gained a crazy amount of followers for a new streamer, and that's what I feel helped kick things off. The cosplay helped me stand out in the directory and people were impressed with the work that had gone into it, and that got me noticed by a lot of people.

THE GAMES

You play a lot of Bungie games—what is it about that company's titles that grabs you?

● For me, it's the perfect combo of games that are fun without being super-realistic—I enjoy other FPS games but they don't grab my interest the way *Halo* and *Destiny* do. The gameplay itself is so smooth and enjoyable, and can be competitive but also fun! Bungie is also historically great at getting involved with its community—the passion of the developers is always so clear.

How do you choose what games you play on stream?

● I just go with the ones that grab my attention and sometimes the games my community seem hyped about. Sometimes there are old

games that are fun to play for nostalgia, like recently we completed a playthrough of *Harry Potter and the Philosopher's Stone*, which was really fun for bringing back childhood memories to a lot of the chat! There are some games I'm not comfortable streaming because I don't think they'd make for entertaining content, and I often come back to *Destiny*, as that's where my community grew from and where many of my stream friends are, but branching out can be fun.

How do you deal with the pressure of having to play well when streaming?

● Sometimes you play well, sometimes you don't! I don't think people realize just how

difficult it is to read the chat while also paying attention to the game. Some days you're just playing poorly for whatever reason, you're distracted or badly coordinated … it happens. If you're not a streamer you can just stop playing and pick it back up another day, but you can't really take a day off streaming just because you're not playing well; so you can either suck it up and wait for the bad plays to pass, or switch games to something less skill-based! There's also the other factor, that for me and most others, Twitch is about being entertaining as much as it is about being good at the games. No one wants to watch a trash player, but if you're playing badly while being entertaining, it's not a big deal. If you and your viewers are having fun that's all that matters—whether that's through your humor or godlike game skills.

STREAMING

How often do you watch other streams? Is there anyone else you particularly like?

● Fairly often! I play *Smite* but enjoy watching other streamers play it more a lot of the time. I enjoy watching Suntouch as he's pretty chill and I can just have him on another screen while I work on other things. Otherwise I watch a lot of *Destiny* streamers because there are a ton of entertaining and friendly people there— including KingGothalion, ProfessorBroman, TripleWreck, and LacedUpLauren, and I love watching Ray aka Brownman for his variety and dry sense of humor.

What's your favorite thing about being a popular streamer?

● I have access to a lot of people and can use that access to help achieve incredible things— like raising money for charity or raise awareness for certain things or people. I can help others achieve success, and due to my perceived popularity (because to me, I'm just a human playing games!), if I reply to someone it often makes their day—so I enjoy knowing I can help make people's days a little better. The world can be a negative place a lot of the time, so being a positive home for a lot of people is a nice feeling.

Conversely, what do you find yourself struggling with as a popular streamer?

● There are so many people who want a piece of you—a personal chat, to play games with you, to feel valued for their support of you, it's just impossible to try and cater to what everyone wants from you and it often leaves people disappointed. That can suck. You never want to disappoint people, but there are only so many hours in a day. That and the fact that so many people will judge you without knowing you at all. You put yourself out there in a way, and people can be very harsh and make snap judgements based on either tiny nuggets of knowledge, or complete hearsay. You have to accept that you're never going to win them all, and people will dislike you just because they can, and they can be very vocal about it, so you have to grow a very thick skin! As a streamer the personality you put out there is going to be a little exaggerated, so people will hate that, which is understandable.

"THERE ARE A TON OF ENTERTAINING AND FRIENDLY PEOPLE THERE"

QUICKFIRE

What is your favorite color?
● Duck-egg blue … like a minty blue green. It's a soothing color!

What is your favorite movie?
● *Scott Pilgrim vs. the World.*

What's your favorite Twitch emote?
● Either PogChamp or OSsloth

What are your hobbies outside of gaming?
● Cosplaying, videography (which was my job before streaming took over my life), and I've been itching to buy a guitar and pick that up again.

If you could change LeahLovesChief to any other username, what would you change it to?
● Absolutely no idea, I'm the worst at naming things.

If you had to play one game for the rest of your life, what would it be?
● *Smite.* So I could get good at it and not suck … eventually. Or *Sonic Adventure 2.*

THE DARK SIDE ... AND THE LIGHT

STAR WARS BATTLEFRONT

Electronic Arts knew it had scored a major win when it acquired the *Star Wars* licensing rights for video games in 2013, and what better way to kick off its run with the series than to resurrect the legendary 2004 shooter franchise *Star Wars Battlefront*? With *Battlefield* developer DICE at the helm, *Star Wars* was reborn in the video game realm, and unsurprisingly, it's become a huge hit.

The game features some of the most iconic scenes from the original *Star Wars* trilogy, making it great for both movie buffs and gamers to watch Let's Plays. Of course, with the game offering you the chance to pilot X-Wings and AT-STs, and take control of famous heroes and villains like Luke Skywalker and Darth Vader, you'll also be eager to jump in yourself to replicate the famous battles you've seen in the films.

DID YOU KNOW?
Star Wars Battlefront featured the largest beta test in EA history, with 9.5 million players logging 1.6 billion minutes.

TOP 3 LET'S PLAY MOMENTS

RIP LUKE SKYWALKER
OCTOBER 9, 2015

1 The Battlefront beta delivered one of the funniest moments ever. A Stormtrooper is watching Luke Skywalker from a distance, taking a few shots with his rifle. Suddenly Luke is on to him and begins his pursuit, the trooper quickly running for his life. Just when Luke is about to deal the killing blow, he is crushed by an AT-AT.

TAKEDOWN, JEDI STYLE
OCTOBER 12, 2015

2 Also from the beta test, one player commanded Luke to use his Force powers for one of the best kills ever. A Stormtrooper trying to take Skywalker down was quickly Force Pushed away, but the poor guy was thrown into a passing TIE Fighter with perfect timing, destroying it. Two for the push of one.

THE POD FROM THE HEAVENS
OCTOBER 8, 2015

3 A Rebel soldier is fending off wave after wave of Imperial forces, and in one particular break in the action, he runs to a small hut at the top of a cliff and awaits a supply drop. The pod soon arrives, but it lands directly on the poor Rebel and kills him instantly. Sometimes even fate is helping the Empire.

BIGGEST LET'S PLAYERS

VILLAINS DEFEATED

"GHOSTROBO"
NAME: ZACH DRAPALA
● NO. OF FOLLOWERS: 1,540,000
● NO. OF VIEWS: 5,500,000

ABOUT: 'GhostRobo' is one of the most prolific Let's Players on YouTube, producing over 5,500 Let's Play videos across multiple games since he began on YouTube in 2010. His *Star Wars Battlefront* playlist has over 5 million hits on its own; he combines gaming skill with a charming sense of humor. He also cohosts the Can't Stop Playing podcast with YouTubers Blitzwinger and VolatileGabe.

HILARIOUSNESS	4
TALKATIVENESS	1
ANGER	4
KNOWLEDGE	5
SKILL	4

JACKFRAGS
NAME: JACK MASON
● NO. OF FOLLOWERS 1,480,000 ● NO. OF VIEWS: 8,700,000

ABOUT: Jack "JackFrags" Mason has been blasting his way through opponents on his YouTube channel since 2012. His *Star Wars Battlefront* videos mix impressive skill at the game with informed analysis of what he's currently showing on-screen. JackFrags's channel is perfect for new *Battlefront* players to learn the ropes.

HILARIOUSNESS	3
TALKATIVENESS	5
ANGER	3
KNOWLEDGE	5
SKILL	4

VIKKSTAR123
NAME: VIKRAM BARN
● NO. OF FOLLOWERS: 477,000 ● NO. OF VIEWS: 3,300,000

ABOUT: What started in 2010 as a small outlet for Let's Play videos quickly blossomed into a premier gaming channel. Vikkstar123 talks as well as he plays, joking and reacting to his games in some hilarious and entertaining ways. He's also a very talented FPS player, showing off some impressive moves throughout his *Battlefront* video series.

HILARIOUSNESS	3
TALKATIVENESS	2
ANGER	4
KNOWLEDGE	3
SKILL	4

LEVELCAPGAMING
NAME: UNKNOWN
● NO. OF FOLLOWERS: 1,400,000 ● NO. OF VIEWS: 332,000,000

ABOUT: When it comes to getting the latest information on *Star Wars Battlefront*, you can't get much better than 'LevelCapGaming'. He's been given early access to *Battlefront* DLC content in the past, meaning you can get an early look at what's coming to the game as he talks you through what you're seeing in a methodical and informative way.

HILARIOUSNESS	1
TALKATIVENESS	3
ANGER	1
KNOWLEDGE	5
SKILL	4

HELL4OPT
NAME: UNKNOWN
● NO. OF FOLLOWERS: 2,000 ● NO. OF VIEWS: 54,000

ABOUT: Why would you want to watch this Russian streamer? Because he's the best *Battlefront* player you'll see in action. While most players storm into the mayhem and see what happens, hell4opt is more cautious, strategically picking apart his opponents from a distance. He's smart, he's clever, and you'll learn a lot watching him play.

HILARIOUSNESS	1
TALKATIVENESS	2
ANGER	1
KNOWLEDGE	5
SKILL	5

AN ALL-STAR THROWDOWN

SUPER SMASH BROS. FOR WII U

Mario vs. Link. Samus vs. Mega Man. Donkey Kong vs. Bowser. *Super Smash Bros.* has settled "Who would win in a fight?" arguments ever since the crossover fighting game series debuted for Nintendo 64 back in 1999. But *Super Smash Bros.* is the biggest of them all. A total of 58 characters make up the roster, which means more dream match-ups than ever before . . . and so

many characters being present means there are some unusual faces in there, like Mr. Game & Watch, Villager and Wii Fitness Trainer.

Many prominent *Smash* players have their own Twitch and YouTube channels, so whether you've been playing since the Nintendo 64 days or if you have just joined the series, these names will help you become the best player you can be.

TOP 3 MOMENTS

CLOUD IS REVEALED
NOVEMBER 12, 2015

1 The mix of *Super Smash Bros.* and *Final Fantasy* was a marriage that no-one expected, but Nintendo surprised us all with the introduction of *Final Fantasy VII*'s hero, Cloud, to *Smash Bros.* Countless reaction videos surfaced soon after, shocked faces and screams of joy filling every one.

ZERO WINS SSB WII U'S FIRST EVO GRAND FINALS
JULY 15, 2015

2 The first appearance of *Super Smash Bros.* at the Evolution Championship Series produced some of the best action of the entire weekend. Chilean player ZeRo walked away with the championship, dominating his opponent Mr. R in the Grand Finals.

"GUY, YOU ARE THE WORST"
DECEMBER 2, 2014

3 Two weeks after the launch of *Super Smash Bros.*, the Smash @ Xanadu tournament hosted one of the strangest matches ever. Guy's Duck Hunt had just launched Pink Fresh's Pit off-screen, only to carelessly run off the stage himself before landing the knockout blow. Pink Fresh won the match, scoring a bizarre victory.

BIGGEST LET'S PLAYERS

ICWOBBLES

NAME: ROBERT WRIGHT
● NO. OF FOLLOWERS: 7,000
● NO. OF VIEWS: 51,000

ABOUT: Although he doesn't have the same viewcount as some of the other players on this list, EVO 2013 runner-up Robert "ICWobbles" Wright is worth checking out. Known for his Ice Climbers play—hence the IC in his name—Robert has also been a commentator for plenty of *Smash* tournaments, making him one of the rare Let's Players who's just as comfortable talking as he is playing. He's currently a member of top team Panda Global Gaming.

HILARIOUSNESS	4
TALKATIVENESS	5
ANGER	4
KNOWLEDGE	5
SKILL	4

SHOFU

NAME: KUNNU SHOFU
● NO. OF FOLLOWERS: 610,000 ● NO. OF VIEWS: 168,000,000

ABOUT: One of the top Fox McCloud players, Shofu not only hosts streams on his personal channel but also appears regularly at the weekly Smash @ Xanadu tournaments hosted in Halethorpe, Maryland, USA. He has placed in the top 10 at 11 of the 27 *Smash Bros.* tournaments he's entered, impressing viewers with fast-paced and relentless Fox skills.

HILARIOUSNESS	3
TALKATIVENESS	3
ANGER	2
KNOWLEDGE	5
SKILL	5

NAIROMK

NAME: NAIROBY QUEZADA
● NO. OF FOLLOWERS: 16,000 ● NO. OF VIEWS: 1,300,000

ABOUT: Nairo is regarded as one of the best *Super Smash Bros.* players in the world, his Zero Suit Samus is nigh unbeatable. His stats in the game speak for themselves: 37 victories in 59 *Super Smash Bros.* tournaments, a third place finish at marquee event EVO 2015, and not a single finish below seventh place on his record.

HILARIOUSNESS	3
TALKATIVENESS	3
ANGER	
KNOWLEDGE	5
SKILL	5

THOMAS J. ASHWELL

NAME: THOMAS J. ASHWELL
● NO. OF FOLLOWERS: 5,500 ● NO. OF VIEWS: 1,700,000

ABOUT: Thomas J. Ashwell's channel isn't exclusively filled wit *Super Smash Bros* videos—he likes to branch out into *Mario* games and some *Splatoon* now and then, too. However, he posts a Super Smash Sundays video every week, so it's the perfect place to get your *Smash* fix. Plus, if you like his work, he has a separate vlog of over 1,000 episodes!

HILARIOUSNESS	2
TALKATIVENESS	
ANGER	1
KNOWLEDGE	
SKILL	

RUSH HOUR SMASH

NAME: RICHARD KING, JR.
● NO. OF FOLLOWERS: 56,000 ● NO. OF VIEWS: 9,800,000

ABOUT: One of the co-creators of *RushHourSmash* tournaments, Keitaro is considered the best Falco player in *Super Smash Bros.* He hosts two major tournament series in the northeast United States: Keitaro's Tournament at Rutgers (KTAR) and Super KTAR. Plus, his Let's Play partner Corey "False" Shin placed in the Top 15 at EVO 2015.

HILARIOUSNESS	4
TALKATIVENESS	5
ANGER	4
KNOWLEDGE	5
SKILL	4

MAKING TRACKS

WORLD OF TANKS

First launched on PC in 2011, free-to-play tank simulator *World of Tanks* has proved a real hit with gamers thanks to its easy-to-master controls, tactical gameplay and huge selection of armored vehicles—and by huge, we mean 390 different tanks to choose from! *WoT* is one of the few games out there that offers hours of fun without making you pay to play, and it's easy to form groups with friends—clans, as they're known—to take to the battlefield. You'll quickly get hooked on the feeling of rumbling towards your opponents with tanks alongside you.

It's also proved a winner for streamers and YouTubers, with average viewer ratings around the 6,500 mark on Twitch. It's remained in the top 30 most popular games, with an especially strong following in Russia. And the best players are called Unicorns—we aren't sure why either!

DID YOU KNOW?
There are over 72,000 clans in *World of Tanks* playing an average of 432,277 battles per day.

STREAMERS' TOP TIPS

KNOW YOUR TANK
Each map is different, so make sure you pick the best tank for the job. "A lot of people pick tanks from the country they come from," says *WoT* expert Oliver Maxfield.

PICK THE RIGHT CLAN
Finding and signing up to a Clan is a great idea to get ahead. "The Clan that suits you best will be the Clan whose goals match your own," says pro player Sybredeth.

LEVEL UP YOUR CREW
Low crew ratings equal poor accuracy, reloading, and aiming speeds. "Select the option 'Accelerate Crew Training' to push all your XP into skilling up your crew," advises The Mighty Jingles.

GETTING INTO POSITION
"Angling your tank properly can significantly increase the chance of an opponent's shell bouncing off your armor," says Nicolas Passemard, head of eSports Europe at Wargaming.

BIGGEST LET'S PLAYERS

THE MIGHTY JINGLES

NAME: PAUL CHARLTON

● NO. OF FOLLOWERS: 460,000
● NO. OF VIEWS: 181,000,000

ABOUT: Paul Charlton, aka The Mighty Jingles, has become one of the main faces of the *World of Tanks* community since 2012. Having spent his younger years serving in the Royal Navy, Paul found the military tactics of *WoT* a perfect fit for his gaming tastes, and his selection of tutorials and tips videos have proved a big hit with the community.

HILARIOUSNESS	3
TALKATIVENESS	
ANGER	1
KNOWLEDGE	4
SKILL	3

QUICKYBABY

NAME: WILL FRAMPTON

● NO. OF FOLLOWERS: 340,000 ● NO. OF VIEWS: 87,200,000

ABOUT: QuickyBaby has become one of the most popular members of the *WOT* community, with his love of the game and livestreams three times a week making him a solid favorite with fans. His regular schedule on Twitch lets him focus on playing matches, while his YouTube channel offers videos tailored to new players and new updates to *WoT*.

HILARIOUSNESS	3
TALKATIVENESS	
ANGER	2
KNOWLEDGE	4
SKILL	4

VSPISHKA

NAME: SERGEY VSPISHKA

● NO. OF FOLLOWERS: 470,000 ● NO. OF VIEWS: 68,900,000

ABOUT: Sergey is one of the faces of the Russian *WOT* scene, and even though he doesn't stream in English, his gameplay is worth studying to pick up essential tips and tricks. Sergey likes to focus on reviewing new tanks, since these new additions make a big difference to the way gamers approach the highly competitive battlefield.

HILARIOUSNESS	2
TALKATIVENESS	4
ANGER	2
KNOWLEDGE	3
SKILL	5

DESERTOD TV

NAME: UNKNOWN

● NO. OF FOLLOWERS: 420,000 ● NO. OF VIEWS: 86,800,000

ABOUT: Russian YouTuber and *WoT* fan Desertod TV likes to split his time between recording gameplay/review videos for YouTube and doing livestreams on Twitch. He streams with other *WoT* players as a party, and his energetic enthusiasm has made him a household name in the *WoT* community, even for those who don't speak Russian!

HILARIOUSNESS	3
TALKATIVENESS	
ANGER	1
KNOWLEDGE	4
SKILL	3

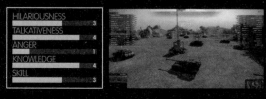

MURAZOR

NAME: UNKNOWN

● NO. OF FOLLOWERS: 460,000 ● NO. OF VIEWS: 99,000,000

ABOUT: Another leading voice in the Russian *WOT* community, Murazor makes videos all about the history and real-life uses of the tanks featured in *WoT*. His videos have proved a huge hit with other fans, and even though he streams in Russian, *WoT* fans should still watch his streams to see his unusual and colorful tanks that he takes into battle.

HILARIOUSNESS	4
TALKATIVENESS	4
ANGER	1
KNOWLEDGE	4
SKILL	3

STAT ATTACK

$500,000
The prize pool for 2016's Capcom Cup.

75 HITS
The biggest combo pulled off so far (using Chun-Li).

STREET FIGHTER V

With its colorful cast of characters and instantly recognizable special moves, the *Street Fighter* series has been entertaining fans for almost 30 years! With *Street Fighter V* now at the forefront of the eSports scene, it doesn't look like that's going to change any time soon!

2,745

The damage you can do with R Mika's Critical Art after fully charging her V-Skill.

Street Fighter V is actually the 25th game in the Street Fighter series.

22

The total size of the roster including all downloadable characters.

OLIVE!

ADVICE FROM THE PROS

ADVICE FROM THE PROS

THESE PEOPLE ARE BECOMING THE
BIGGEST NAMES IN GAMING. HERE
THEY SHARE SOME OF THEIR SECRETS
ON THEIR RISE TO THE TOP …

What advice would you give to someone on how to get more YouTube or Twitch fans?

ZEGOATTT

If you have just started streaming and you get discouraged by a low viewer count, stop paying attention to the numbers. For me, personally, when I stopped paying attention to numbers like followers and viewer count, and started focusing on my community, that was when I felt "closer" to my stream. After that, my regular viewer and subscriber count started to grow naturally as well. People like to feel welcomed and appreciated, so for me, growing a positive community is the number-one thing when it comes to livestreaming. The second thing I suggest is putting effort into social media as well as your Twitch stream. With social media, you can connect to your viewers on a personal level by sharing moments from your life outside the streams, and you can also connect and network with other streamers. And the last tip that I want to give is to relax and avoid being negative, like being jealous of other people's success. Everybody is on their own path of going toward their goals, and you should not compare yourself to others—just be happy about their success and learn as much as you can from them. Take their success as an inspiration not discouragement. Believe in yourself.

ZEGOATTT
FROM RIGA, LATVIA
30,000 FANS
Up and coming streamer for competitive games

> **"For me, growing a positive community is the number-one thing when it comes to livestreaming"**

ADVICE FROM THE PROS

What would you say to someone deciding which games to stream on Twitch or record for YouTube?

DEFEAT

KILLED BY
MrMonkeyDeamond

REACH A SCORE OF 1000
1000 SCORE

MRMEOLA

Choosing which games to record for YouTube can be a quite difficult thing to do! I like to think it comes down to the individual, the player, the person who is going to be experiencing it firsthand. Choosing a game to play is almost like picking what to eat on a restaurant menu—so many meals sound good, but you can only pick one. If you're like me, you usually order something you know you will enjoy. Today there are SO MANY games available to us, it can be really hard to choose what to play! Similar to food, we tend to have our own individual tastes in gaming. Someone may enjoy first-person shooters like *Halo*, others prefer RPGs like *Final Fantasy*, others prefer platformers like *Super Mario* and *Sonic*. The most important thing about making videos is having fun, so you need to pick games that you will enjoy. I really enjoy being creative, and recently there have been a lot of games that let me create things: games like *Minecraft*, *Scrap Mechanic*, *Terraria*, or *Ark: Survival Evolved*. They let you play games the way you want, and I think this is a very important thing when it comes to YouTube. It lets your videos be much more unique, it lets you be creative, and usually means your videos will be different to everyone else's.

MRMEOLA
FROM ADELAIDE, AUSTRALIA
203,000 FANS
One of the most energetic and enthusiastic gamers on YouTube

"Today there are SO MANY games available to us, it can be really hard to choose what to play!"

What's the best way to deal with negative feedback?

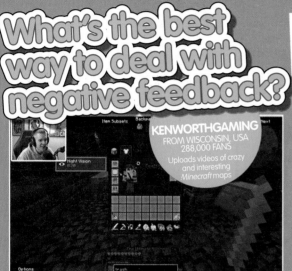

KENWORTHGAMING
FROM WISCONSIN, USA
288,000 FANS
Uploads videos of crazy and interesting *Minecraft* maps

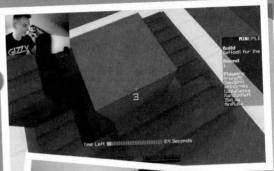

KENWORTHGAMING

I try not to think of it as negative feedback but more as constructive criticism. Of course there will be those comments that are 100 per cent negative, but I just try to hover past those! Honestly, though, the Internet is sometimes just a tough place for anyone, but especially people whose lives are within and around YouTube. Most of the time, unless you did something that you shouldn't have, the positive feedback is a lot stronger than the negative, and I try to focus my attention on that.

WHYBEARE
FROM CALIFORNIA, USA
524,000 FANS
Specializes in epic car crashes for driving games

GIZZY GAZZA
FROM LONDON, ENGLAND
1,173,000 FANS
Creates stories in *Minecraft* and shares them with the world

WHYBEARE

I deal with negative feedback as objectively as possible. If the criticism is something like "You suck," I just ignore it because it does nothing to make future content better. But if the criticism talks about something specific that I have control over, I will usually consider what they are saying. If I disagree with their criticism I might state my opinion, or do nothing at all. For those just starting out, I would suggest that you do what you think will make the best video possible, and only listen to the critics if you feel what they are saying could help you make better content. If someone is just insulting you, there really isn't much to gain from starting a conversation with them, so just ignore them or block them if you feel you must do something. You probably started doing this for fun, don't let other people ruin that.

When all is said and done, what do you enjoy most about being a streamer?

GIZZYGAZZA

Most definitely having the chance in life to fly around the world to meet those who love my channel and videos. Meeting the people who helped make the life you live and to thank them is one of life's many treasures. Never give up! Success doesn't happen overnight, so be sure you keep at it. I've been doing YouTube videos regularly for six years, and my YouTube channel is ten years old. Be sure you enjoy it too; never do it just to be popular, because the content won't turn out that good.

GAME PROFILE

CREATING YOUR OWN GAMING HISTORY

SUPER MARIO MAKER

That bright red hat, that bushy moustache and that cheeky smile … after 30 years of helping him slip and slide through some of the best levels ever created, Mario has rightfully earned his place as the most recognizable character in gaming. But have you ever thought that *you* could do better? That Nintendo's levels are good, but not nearly as good as your own ideas for unique and challenging levels?

Super Mario Maker gives you a chance to scratch that creative itch, mixing up Mario elements like Goombas, warp pipes, Question Blocks, and more in brand new ways. After you've made your levels, they can be uploaded for other people to download, play, and review, so there's a never-ending stream of new creations to enjoy. Think you can do better than legendary Mario creator Shigeru Miyamoto? Here's your chance …

DID YOU KNOW?

Super Mario Maker was released 30 years after *Super Mario Bros.*, the biggest-selling Mario game ever made.

TOP 3 STREAM MOMENTS

DAD VS. MOM
SEPTEMBER 16, 2015

1 It's nice when parents can find a game to play with their children … or without. Dad vs. Mom features the parents from FGTeeV facing off against one another across various challenges. The stream was ample evidence that 1) parents are not that bad at games, and 2) competitiveness doesn't wear off as you get older.

U-BREAK
NOVEMBER 3, 2015

2 PangaeaPanga likes to create difficult levels. No, seriously, *really* difficult levels. U-Break is one of the very toughest, which was made clear when PangaeaPanga tried playing through his ruthless creation. Death is constant. It's funny, silly, and shows just how dramatically one person can torment himself.

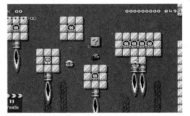

THE IMPOSSIBLE RUN
SEPTEMBER 18, 2015

3 Hosted by TheDiamondMinecart, the theme of this streaming session is to make it through an intensely tough set of levels. The difficulty slowly cranks up with each level and ends with a fiery showdown against Bowser. The stream has since been uploaded to YouTube, where it has racked up two million views.

BIGGEST STREAMERS

TRIHEX
NAME: MYCHAL JEFFERSON
- NO. OF FOLLOWERS: **22,000**
- NO. OF VIEWS: **2,600,000**

ABOUT: Trihex made his name conquering *Jet Set Radio* levels in record time. More recently, however, he has set his sights on making *Super Mario Maker* look easy. He's also a dedicated weightlifter and gives bodybuilding tips during his *Mario* Let's Plays; it's the combination of gaming skills and life skills that makes him so unique. Working on Mario levels *and* working on our biceps? Why not!

CREATIVITY	2
HUMOR	3
FRIENDLINESS	3
CHATTINESS	4
KNOWLEDGE	4

STAMPYLONGHEAD
NAME: JOSEPH GARRETT
- NO. OF FOLLOWERS: **7,200,000**
- NO. OF VIEWS: **4,800,000,000**

ABOUT: Stampy might be better known for his *Minecraft* and *Terraria* Let's Plays, but he's also completed his fair share of *Super Mario Maker* levels as well. Stampy's Let's Plays are always fun and cheerful, even if he's taking on the hardest levels and struggling to complete them. It's also kind of funny hearing him laughing at the weird levels!

CREATIVITY	2
HUMOR	4
FRIENDLINESS	5
CHATTINESS	5
KNOWLEDGE	

PTKEN
NAME: XIAO WEN
- NO. OF FOLLOWERS: **1,100**
- NO. OF VIEWS: **115,000**

ABOUT: Xiao Wen is from Taiwan, and he mainly speaks Chinese—but don't let that stop you from watching his Let's Plays. There might not be another player better than Ptken currently playing any *Mario* game. His *Mario Maker* sessions are a master class in how to be the best platform player you can possibly be, and the skill on display is incredible.

CREATIVITY	2
HUMOR	1
FRIENDLINESS	4
CHATTINESS	4
KNOWLEDGE	5

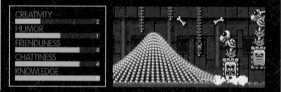

IATEYOURPIE
NAME: CALEB BLOOMER
- NO. OF FOLLOWERS: **67,000**
- NO. OF VIEWS: **7,500,000**

ABOUT: IAteYourPie is the originator of Mario Maker Mondays, a popular competition in which level creators submit their designs and players compete to finish them as quickly as possible. The top 16 best finishers are awarded points, which are added up over the weeks that make up a season until an overall champion is crowned.

CREATIVITY	3
HUMOR	2
FRIENDLINESS	5
CHATTINESS	4
KNOWLEDGE	4

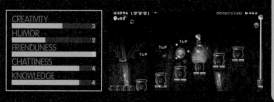

WITWIX
NAME: TOM BURKE
- NO. OF FOLLOWERS: **67,000**
- NO. OF VIEWS: **1,900,000**

ABOUT: While most *Super Mario Maker* Let's Players dabble between creating levels and playing through them, WitWix focuses on conquering creations made by other players. He looks for the unique and challenging levels to tackle, which makes his channel worth watching if you're struggling to find interesting *Super Mario Maker* levels yourself.

CREATIVITY	1
HUMOR	5
FRIENDLINESS	3
CHATTINESS	5
KNOWLEDGE	4

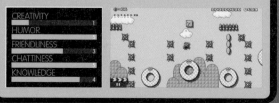

BACK OF THE NET!

FIFA 16

Soccer is by far the most popular sport in the world, so it's no surprise that *FIFA* is the most popular sports video game.

After all, for those of us that love the beautiful game, *FIFA* is the closest we are ever going to get to scoring spectacular goals while being cheered on by an excited crowd. With its realistically re-created players and stadiums, official licensing,

and brilliant matchday-style presentation, *FIFA* does everything it can to let us taste what it is like to be a soccer superstar who can dazzle fans with a soccer ball at their feet.

Of course, along with the experience, we also want to win! And what better way to learn how to do just that than by watching the best in the world and seeing what you can add to your game.

DID YOU KNOW?

In the first 16 days after *FIFA 16*'s release, 693 million goals were scored in the 326 million games played.

STREAMERS' TOP TIPS

FORMATION IS KEY
Play a formation that suits you and stick with it; a different formation and line-up for every game can be detrimental. Know your players and use them to the best of their abilities.

WATCH & LEARN
Conceding an early goal isn't good. Figure out your opponent's tactics and style of play in those first few crucial minutes before taking the game to them and exploiting their weaknesses.

USE FINESSE
The best way to score in *FIFA 16* is through mastery of Finesse Shots. If you find yourself hurtling towards the goal and a one-on-one with the keeper, simply finesse it in the corner.

DON'T BE GREEDY
In *FIFA 16*, you need to pass the ball around to succeed. In a tricky match, the Driven Pass makes it really easy to switch the ball or play a ball through the middle to your striker.

BIGGEST ESPORTS PLAYERS

HUGE GORILLA
NAME: SPENCER EALING
● **WINS:** Vice ESWC Champion 2015, three-time Gfinity Champion
● **AGE:** 19

ABOUT: Representing the Epsilon eSports team, Huge Gorilla is a three-time Gfinity Champion, nabbing wins at the Spring Masters, Play Like a Legend Season One, and Play Like a Legend Grand Finals, despite only playing *FIFA* for just over two years. That Huge Gorilla has had so much success in such a short time suggests there's still more to come from a player already considered one of the best around.

SOCCER SILLINESS 2
PITCH RAGE 2
TALKATIVENESS 2
PITCH SKILLS 5
PLAYER MANAGEMENT 3

DAVID BYTHEWAY
NAME: DAVID BYTHEWAY
○ **WINS:** Runner-up, FIWC Brazil 2014 ○ **AGE:** 23

ABOUT: David Bytheway is considered by many to be one of the greatest people operating in the *FIFA* community due to his success over recent years. His reputation has only been enhanced by the fact that he was signed by German Bundesliga club Wolfsburg to represent the club in the pro FIFA scene, blurring the lines between sport and video games.

SOCCER SILLINESS 1
PITCH RAGE 2
TALKATIVENESS 4
PITCH SKILLS 4
PLAYER MANAGEMENT 4

AUGUST ROSENMEIER
NAME: AUGUST ROSENMEIER
● **WINS:** FIWC 2014 Champion, ESWC 2015 Champion ● **AGE:** 20

ABOUT: Rosenmeier is a five-time Danish National Champion, four-time Scandinavian champion, and two-time World Champion. He started playing *FIFA* when he was eight years old. Since then he has transformed himself into one of the best players in the world, eventually beating David Bytheway in the FIFA Interactive World Cup Brazil in 2014.

SOCCER SILLINESS 1
PITCH RAGE 2
TALKATIVENESS 3
PITCH SKILLS 4
PLAYER MANAGEMENT 3

MR DONE
NAME: ABDULAZIZ ALSHEHRI
● **WINS:** FIWC World Cup 2015 Champion, three-time Middle East & Asia Champion ● **AGE:** 24

ABOUT: Having started playing *FIFA* in 2009, he qualified for the semi-finals in the 2013 FIFA Interactive World Cup. He won the tournament in 2015 in Munich, Germany, and has since been crowned a four-time Saudi Arabia Champion and three-time Middle East & Asia Champion.

SOCCER SILLINESS 3
PITCH RAGE 2
TALKATIVENESS 3
PITCH SKILLS 1
PLAYER MANAGEMENT 4

JULIANOOO
NAME: JULIEN DASSONVILLE
○ **WINS:** Vice FIWC Champion 2015 ○ **AGE:** 25

ABOUT: Currently ranked number two in the world, Dassonville lost the top spot in 2015 to Abdulaziz Alsherhi. The Frenchman holds a number of accolades, including titles in France, Europe, and Reflex GT. He started playing in 2009, qualifying for three FIFA Interactive World Cup Grand Finals, and cites Stoke City as one of his favorite teams to play as.

SOCCER SILLINESS 2
PITCH RAGE 2
TALKATIVENESS 2
PITCH SKILLS 4
PLAYER MANAGEMENT 3

ALL THE RIGHT MOVES
MADDEN NFL 16

W ith the passion and love that America's favorite sport inspires in its fans, it's fortunate that there's a way to get your fix of football without having to wait for next week's round of games.

Madden NFL lets you take control of your favorite team to relive their glories, avenge their defeats, and take them on fantasy runs to victory at the Super Bowl.

The series' trademark realism—something that's been in Madden NFL's DNA since day one, thanks to legendary coach John Madden's involvement with the game—means that it brilliantly recreates the competitive spirit you see on the field when you play against friends.

With millions of combined views, these expert streamers' weekly hints, tips and tricks can help you dominate your buddies on the playing field.

DID YOU KNOW?
The first game took four years to develop because of John Madden's insistence that it be as realistic as possible.

STREAMERS' TOP TIPS

STRONG CLOSE— QUICK TOSS
Simply select Quick Toss, run the play, and then follow your blockers and take the ball upfield. This one works best with a speedy running back and solid offensive line to grind out yards.

DON'T FORGET THE PASS
Don't run with the ball just for the sake of it. Instead, make frequent use of passing plays. This is especially effective when playing online since passing plays are harder to defend than running plays.

CATCH IT IF YOU CAN
There are three types of catches, each one producing different results. Try using the sideline catch if you're losing toward the end of the game since you'll need to take the ball out of bounds to stop the clock and save valuable time.

DEFENSIVE KING
If you're losing and your opponent has the ball, think about regularly starting a pass rusher. As well as giving your defensive game some order, it can seriously improve your chances of a killer interception that leads to a win.

BIGGEST STRLAMERS

CHRIS SMOOVE

NAME: CHRIS SMOOVE

● NO. OF FOLLOWERS: 2,900,000
● NO. OF VIEWS: 1,120,000,000

ABOUT: Formerly known as Smoove7182954, this American superstar gamer is famous for both his *Madden* and *NBA 2K* skills, as well as his gloriously cheesy auto-tuned catchphrase, "SPLASH!" If you've just started streaming games yourself, make sure you listen to how Chris Smoove manages to pull listeners in and build excitement through his commentary, which gets louder and more frantic to match the on-screen action of the game he's playing!

HILARIOUSNESS	3
MADDEN-NESS	4
COMMENTARY	4
PLAYBOOK KNOWLEDGE	4
MADD SKILLZ	4

QJB

NAME: QJ BRIDGES

● NO. OF FOLLOWERS: 650,000 ● NO. OF VIEWS: 145,000,000

ABOUT: QJB is a wildly entertaining YouTuber who hurls out high-octane, non-stop, action-packed gameplay—not just from *Madden*, but from a raft of other titles too, including *NBA 2K*, *NCAA*, and *MLB The Show*. The guy's an entertainer who doles out countless gameplay feeds infused with slick beats, pro tips, and gaming news.

HILARIOUSNESS	4
MADDEN-NESS	4
COMMENTARY	4
PLAYBOOK KNOWLEDGE	4
MADD SKILLZ	4

CULLENBURGER

NAME: CULLENBURGER

● NO. OF FOLLOWERS: 395,000 ● NO. OF VIEWS: 95,000,000

ABOUT: Cullenburger has been streaming videos on YouTube since 2012, specializing in delivering a massive roster of *Madden* and *NBA* tips and tricks, all delivered with his trademark machine-gun-paced style of narration. In fact, he speaks so fast that you may need to watch his videos twice to understand exactly what he is saying!

HILARIOUSNESS	2
MADDEN-NESS	4
COMMENTARY	4
PLAYBOOK KNOWLEDGE	3
MADD SKILLZ	3

TOKENASTY

NAME: TOKE

● NO. OF FOLLOWERS: 300,000 ● NO. OF VIEWS: 56,000,000

ABOUT: He originally launched his own YouTube channel as MaddenGOAT, before dropping that title and releasing videos under the new name of ToKeNasty. To date he's amassed himself a huge following of fans on the streaming site, as well as 50,000 followers on Twitch, where he regularly rolls out a series of hilarious streams for *Madden*.

HILARIOUSNESS	4
MADDEN-NESS	4
COMMENTARY	4
PLAYBOOK KNOWLEDGE	3
MADD SKILLZ	4

ANTODABOSS

NAME: ANTO GARABET

● NO. OF FOLLOWERS: 550,000 ● NO. OF VIEWS: 170,000,000

ABOUT: AntoDaBoss has been on the streaming scene since 2009, populating his feeds with pro tips for *Madden* and *NBA*, as well as producing his own chat show called The Boss Talks, where he takes part in ridiculously crafted challenges. He also uploads videos of his visits to real NFL games and even has his own clothing line called Boss Nation.

HILARIOUSNESS	3
MADDEN-NESS	2
COMMENTARY	3
PLAYBOOK KNOWLEDGE	4
MADD SKILLZ	3

HOW TO BE A ...
SHOUTCASTER

SHOUTCASTER is the term for someone who commentates on online gameplay

JAMES "JZFB" BARDOLPH
OF FACEIT MEDIA

Whether it's picking shoutcasters for shows, fixing technical issues, helping staff on and behind the camera, sorting out disputes between teams, or shoutcasting himself, James Bardolph has seen it all. Here, he shares his unique knowledge and wisdom on how to get started in the world of shoutcasting and becoming one of the best ...

CREATING TENSION

In games where the viewer has complete information and the player does not—FPS games where you can see where all the players are, for example—you know in advance when something big will happen. Focus on those moments!

DEEP KNOWLEDGE

Former pros aside, it is common for casters to be terrible at the games on which they commentate. Many can try to sound intelligent by saying "this team does x, that team does y," but that does not really demonstrate one's own intelligence at the game. I usually study replays, and learn styles and tendencies.

BUILD A STORY

My main objective is to give the viewer something to care about by giving the recent history between the players and teams. Have they recently played each other? Does one team have more pressure to win?

TIME TO GO NUTS

One of the key things to recognize is when the action has reached a crescendo—it's all going down and commentary needs to reflect that. When things are going nuts, that's when I go nuts!

WHEN TO STAY QUIET

You don't need to be talking all the time. For casters, it's important to understand how dead air can contribute. One mistake I often see is casters talking to stream when doing professional casts. This is just wrong! It detracts from the commentary and atmosphere.

DIFFERENT SHOUTCASTING STYLES

EXCITABLE
Notable Example: ODPixel (*Dota 2*)
These shoutcasters will provide lightning-fast, play-by-play commentary before exploding with excitement at critical moments of the match they're watching. The energy is infectious and their ability to keep up with the action is what makes them so entertaining.

INFORMATIVE
Notable Example: Artosis *(Hearthstone)*
With expert insight into statistics and strategy, informative shoutcasters work best as backup to the play-by-play commentator, pointing out secret tricks or mentioning cool facts about the player's history that you might have otherwise missed.

FORMER PLAYER
Notable Example: Seth Killian (*Street Fighter*)
It makes sense that former high-level players make the leap into shoutcasting—they know the game inside out, they automatically have respect thanks to their playing history and they can afford to commentate at a slower pace because their words carry more weight.

GET FEEDBACK

Always get feedback. This is the main way to improve! It's also important to have another caster who you can bounce ideas off and give honest, frank feedback to each other. Also, watching casts to spot bad habits is very useful.

LIVE CASTING

Commentating live is different from bedroom casting. Generally speaking, don't get excited for the sake of getting excited—is what's happening important? Unusual? Always have perspective.

WHAT MAKES A SUCCESSFUL SHOUTCASTER?

DO YOUR RESEARCH

Looking up the players and teams you're shoutcasting on before the match begins means during quiet moments, you'll have something to talk about.

QUICK TALKING

One skill you'll have to practice is talking quickly but clearly, so you can keep up when a critical moment happens in the match you're shoutcasting.

DEALING WITH NERVES

A huge part of being a great shoutcaster is overcoming nerves and being confident with your delivery. Don't stress though, this comes with experience!

GAME EXPERIENCE

Whatever game you've focused on, keep playing and practicing! You need to keep up with the latest tactics and game updates.

LOTS OF TRAVEL

If you want to carve out your own career in shoutcasting, you'll have to travel to tournaments and events all around the world.

THE WINNER TAKES IT ALL

During the winning moment, it is common to close out the commentary with a few words then leave the mic dead for viewers to enjoy the images. This is how sports broadcasts deal with these moments as well.

BE YOURSELF

This is crucial. People need a reason to be interested. No-one wants to listen to someone who says or does the same things as everyone else. It's important casters are themselves without making the show about themselves and that they aren't afraid to have an opinion.

YOUR BEST FRIEND
Notable Example: James Bardolph (*Street Fighter*)
Some shoutcasters successfully combine a laidback and relaxed style with their own lingo and in-jokes, which makes you feel as though you've been friends with them forever and part of a unique club. Only the most charismatic of shoutcasters can pull this off!

FAN FRIENDLY
Notable Example: Forsen (*Hearthstone*)
Some shoutcasters will talk back to their fans during games, responding to questions or reading out funny comments live on the stream. This helps create a friendly atmosphere—it feels like you've been invited into their home and made to feel welcome!

QUIRKY
Notable Example: Chris Hu (*Street Fighter*)
Sometimes, shoutcasters are so different and unique that you can't really put them in a category with anyone else. It might be their sense of humor, their catchphrases, their unique delivery … but there will be something that makes them memorable.

HERE COMES THE PAIN (AND THE HADOUKENS)

STREET FIGHTER V

When it comes to one-to-one fighting, the *Street Fighter* series is the big daddy. It's the purest form of competition there is, as you take on your opponent in a battle of wits, skill, and nerve. What makes Street Fighter so special is that each match up feels unique. Can Russian grappler Zangief get close enough to the defense specialist Dhalism to land his bone-crushing throws? Can wrestler R. Mika force the agile and elusive Rashid towards the corner, where she can land combos?

The latest addition to the series, *Street Fighter V*, makes these match-ups even more interesting by giving each character awesome V-Skill moves—Ken can run at his opponent, for example, while M. Bison can reflect any projectiles thrown at him by his opponents, like Ryu's famous hadouken fireballs! Whether it's studying the match-ups or simply watching two brilliant players taking each other on, *Street Fighter V* is a glorious spectacle that feels like it's been tailor-made for Twitch.

TOP 3 LET'S PLAY MOMENTS

SNAKE EYEZ BEATS A BOT
FEBRUARY 27, 2016

1 When Darryl "Snake Eyez" Lewis came across a player called "tool_assisted-v4" in an online match, it was clear that he was playing a "bot," or AI-controlled character. The opponent had an unbelieveable streak of 274 consecutive wins, but Snake Eyez's Zangief unleashed a massive V-Trigger to break the streak and beat the bot!

ZANGIEF SCALPS A PRO
OCTOBER 10, 2015

2 After the first round ends in a double KO, Zangief expert RB Snake Eyez faces Japanese pro superstar Kazunoko in a tense final round. Using the speedy Karin, Kazunoko takes an early lead, but Snake Eyez overcomes the slowness of his big Russian grappler to pound his opponent into defeat.

CHUN LI BLOWS RYU AWAY
AUGUST 15, 2015

3 Having matched up online with a random player who knew how to deal serious damage with Ryu, YouTuber and aspiring pro gamer RajmanGaming settled on one of his favorite fighters—Chinese brawler Chun Li. He hits him with a bold low kick, then throws a blue fireball that wins the fight in nail-biting style.

BIGGEST LET'S PLAYERS

SNAKE EYEZ

NAME: DARRYL S. LEWIS

- NO. OF FOLLOWERS: 30,000
- NO. OF VIEWS: 295,000

ABOUT: Some *Street Fighter* players are known as character specialists—they pick one character and stick with them through the highs and the lows. Snake Eyez is the most famous character specialist of them all. His Zangief is feared by all opponents, as Snake Eyez is a master at closing down distance and getting to close range where he can do the most damage. His streams are a masterclass in how to make the most of your character's unique strengths.

HILARIOUSNESS	2
ANGER	2
TALKATIVENESS	4
KNOWLEDGE	4
SKILL	4

VESPERARCADE

NAME: GORDON HANCOCK

- NO. OF FOLLOWERS: 55,000
- NO. OF VIEWS: 23,600,000

ABOUT: Vesper joined YouTube in 2009 and soon started uploading videos focused on the *Street Fighter* franchise. He also used to stream a lot on Twitch, but now he mostly uses YouTube as his main platform for uploading and streaming. His videos focus on news updates and combo tutorials as well as showcasing his online matches.

HILARIOUSNESS	2
ANGER	2
TALKATIVENESS	3
KNOWLEDGE	4
SKILL	4

INFILTRATION85

NAME: LEE SEON-WOO

- NO. OF FOLLOWERS: 42,000
- NO. OF VIEWS: 280,000

ABOUT: Although he doesn't stream in English, you won't be tuning into Infiltration's stream for the chat. Instead, you'll be watching the world's best *Street Fighter V* player at the peak of his powers. Watching Infiltration pick apart his opponents with elaborate combos is an absolute joy and shows just what's possible at the highest level of play in Capcom's game.

HILARIOUSNESS	1
ANGER	1
TALKATIVENESS	2
KNOWLEDGE	5
SKILL	5

EG JWONG

NAME: JUSTIN WONG

- NO. OF FOLLOWERS: 116,000
- NO. OF VIEWS: 4,100,000

ABOUT: Justin Wong is a fighting games legend, having won multiple tournaments for games like *Ultimate Marvel vs. Capcom 3*, *Skullgirls*, and *Ultimate Street Fighter IV*. So it's no surprise to see Justin playing *Street Fighter V*, and listening to him break down matches into what went right and what went wrong provides valuable insight for players of all levels.

HILARIOUSNESS	2
ANGER	3
TALKATIVENESS	2
KNOWLEDGE	5
SKILL	5

RUNJDRUN

NAME: JOHN DAVID WITHERSPOON

- NO. OF FOLLOWERS: 161,000
- NO. OF VIEWS: 17,200,000

ABOUT: RunJDrun, aka John David Witherspoon, is a film editor, comedian, and professional gamer who first opened a channel in 2010. He runs multiple channels, from daily vlogs, comedy sketches, and video-game playthroughs. He's is a huge fan of *Street Fighter V*, but his channel also covers plenty of new and retro releases.

HILARIOUSNESS	4
ANGER	3
TALKATIVENESS	4
KNOWLEDGE	3
SKILL	3

WHICH CHARACTER
WILL YOU CHOOSE?

STREAMERS' TOP PICKS

ZANGIEF

PLAYER NAME: Snake Eyez
FIGHTING STYLE: Russian/American pro wrestling

LEVELS

POWER:	5
MOBILITY:	1
TECHNIQUE:	2
HEALTH:	5
RANGE:	3

CRITICAL ART:
Bolshoi Russian Suplex—burly brawler Zangief's Critical Art is, unsurprisingly, straight out of the pro-wrestling handbook. He grabs his opponent around the chest and performs a devastating German Suplex, a highly damaging move.

RYU

PLAYER NAME: Daigo Umehara
FIGHTING STYLE: Ansatsuken

LEVELS

POWER:	4
MOBILITY:	3
RANGE:	2
TECHNIQUE:	3
HEALTH:	3

CRITICAL ART:
Shinku Hadoken—the bandana-wearing fighter's Critical Art gathers up lots of blue energy while black-and-white smoke circles him. He then unleashes a super-powerful Shinku Hadoken fireball. If Denjin mode is activated, this fireball will electrocute your opponent as well.

STREAMERS' TOP TIPS

MASTER THE COUNTER
"Instead of acting like a normal counter, a Crush Counter is more like a retaliation that doubles the damage of hard strikes," says YouTuber TWBGreatness.

HIT THOSE COMBOS
Chaining combos is one of the most important elements when playing. "Always be willing to sacrifice some of your own health in pursuit of a combo," advises Snake Eyez.

THINK WITH V-GAUGE
V-Gauge offers powerful new moves. "Some characters have three bars, while others only have two, and each one will have unique V-Reversals and V-Triggers," says VesperArcade.

COUNT THOSE FRAMES
If you want to become a pro player, studying frame data is really important. "Knowing where a character's hurt box is will help you chain better combos," adds Snake Eyez.

BIRDIE

PLAYER NAME: LPN
FIGHTING STYLE: Bar room brawling/pro wrestling

LEVELS

POWER:	5
RANGE:	4
TECHNIQUE:	3
HEALTH:	5
MOBILITY:	1

CRITICAL ART: Skip To My Chain—Birdie lunges forward and wraps his opponent up in steel chains, performing two "jump ropes" before smiling and throwing them back to the ground. It's definitely one of the most stylish moves in *Street Fighter V*.

CHUN-LI

PLAYER NAME: Justin Wong
FIGHTING STYLE: Chinese martial arts

LEVELS

POWER:	2
HEALTH:	2
MOBILITY:	5
RANGE:	4
TECHNIQUE:	5

CRITICAL ART: Houyoku Sen—Chun-Li lunges towards her opponent and hits them with a high kick followed by a crossover kick. She then unleashes a flurry of Hyakuretsukyaku (fast kicks known as Lightning Kicks). If these connect, she'll finish with a final kick that sends her opponent soaring.

CAMMY

PLAYER NAME: Kenryo "Mago" Hayashi
FIGHTING STYLE: Shadaloo and special forces training

LEVELS

POWER:	3
HEALTH:	2
MOBILITY:	5
RANGE:	3
TECHNIQUE:	2

CRITICAL ART: Cross Stinger Assault—Cammy jumps into the air and hits a Cannon Strike (a powerful downward kick). If the hit is unblocked, Cammy will launch her opponent into the air, hit them with more kicks, and finish them off with a Spiral Arrow (a lunging corkscrew kick).

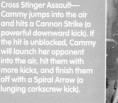

PRO INTERVIEW

AVEN BIRD

Aven Bird, aka TS_Shinji, is a British eSports gamer who competes competitively in *Street Fighter V*. He's currently a part of Team Senses, based in Manchester.

What was it about *Street Fighter V* that attracted you to it?
I enjoy the basics in a fighting game, and *Street Fighter V* boils down to it at its core. There is a huge range of great fighting games along with communities for them for newcomers to pick up and play, which is the great thing about this current generation of fighting games.

How different does *SFV* feel compared to *Ultra Street Fighter IV*? Has your playstyle changed to account for new characters?
From my own experiences with *SFV*, I feel like it's a lot different from *USFIV* in terms of the speed of the games—it's not so much about being scared of being knocked down anymore. The game has given you a good amount of options to wake up with (when your character gets up off the floor).

You're part of the growing competitive scene in Manchester—tell us what's it like being part of that gaming community?
If it wasn't for gaming communities like mine growing, and the rest of the ones in the UK, we wouldn't have these fantastic major tournaments you see every year now, including the great Capcom Pro Tour events. I also wouldn't have had the chance to show off my own ability at tournaments, which eventually led to me getting sponsored by Team Senses (@TeamSenses on Twitter).

Do you have a YouTube or Twitch account? If so, how has having these platforms changed how you play/interact?
Having the ability to use a platform like YouTube alone is incredible; you literally are given the ability to watch the biggest fighting game events of the year in any country. People upload an enormous amount of content on YT purely just to show off character technology they have found out, or even just tutorials with each character to help new players learn them.

What's your advice for gamers who want to play *Street Fighter V* competitively?
Try and play the best you can play as much as possible; even if you are being beaten you will come out of it learning something every single time. Always record your losses against good players—watch them back and see what you're doing wrong.

MODERN FAMILY VALUES

THE SIMS

Very few games can compete with *The Sims* when it comes to sheer popularity and diversity of audience. Whereas most games ask you to kill, destroy, and fight your way to success, *The Sims* is all about careful consideration and thoughtful progress in your bid to provide a virtual family with as great a life as you possibly can.

This framework has meant that publisher Electronic Arts has been able to proudly boast that the franchise has racked up over 175 million sales since it was first launched in 2000. So it's no surprise that *The Sims* enjoys a vast and healthy community of streamers broadcasting their daily experiences with the game. If you're looking for some tips and ideas, or if you just want to ogle at some creatively designed houses and laugh at hilariously dysfunctional virtual families, these are the people to look up and start following.

DID YOU KNOW?

The Sims 3 sold an incredible 10 million copies! It is one of only eight games to ever do so.

TOP 3 LET'S PLAY MOMENTS

FOUR IMMORTAL SISTERS
MARCH 10, 2015

1 This video series from Vixella tells the story of four sisters who live in a unique house with four separate wings connected by courtyards. Each sister lives in one of the wings, and each episode tells her story. Despite the title, the sisters eventually die—although how the survivors deal with the pain is a highlight.

MODERN DESERT BLAZE
JANUARY 28, 2015

2 Speed builds are creation videos that have been sped up, and this is one of the best examples. Here LifeSimmer takes you through the creation of an elaborate, white-walled house built in the desert heat; it shows how to achieve everything from the initial foundations to the interior decorating details.

HERE COMES THE BABY!
MAY 9, 2016

3 If you haven't been following Deligracy's Sorority House series, you're missing out. In this episode, two of the sisters go out to the park together. However, one of them is about to have a baby, and when the baby starts coming the two friends have to rush to the hospital! Thankfully, a lovely baby girl, called Indigo, is born.

BIGGEST LET'S PLAYERS

LIFESIMMER

NAME: CHRISTINA SARAKAS
● NO. OF FOLLOWERS: 718,000
● NO. OF VIEWS: 178,100,000

ABOUT: A prolific creator of *The Sims* content, LifeSimmer releases two to three videos every week dedicated to her experiences with the games. Her videos cover everything from the latest expansion packs to her reviews of the full games, as well as giveaways and regular episodes on her Sims working lives. She also creates Q&A videos to help fans of the game and detail more about her life.

HILARIOUSNESS	4
TALKATIVENESS	
ANGER	1
KNOWLEDGE	3
CREATIVITY	3

VIXELLA

NAME: SASHA
● NO. OF FOLLOWERS: 330,000 ● NO. OF VIEWS: 45,200,000

ABOUT: Previously known as "FancySimmer," Vixella has been creating *The Sims* Let's Plays since early 2014. She's gained popularity through her house-building and create-a-Sim videos, highlighting her interest in construction. Her building skills have come from lots of practice, so it's no surprise to see her showcasing her building expertise in *Minecraft*, too.

HILARIOUSNESS	2
TALKATIVENESS	4
ANGER	1
KNOWLEDGE	4
CREATIVITY	4

THESIMSUPPLY

NAME: JAMES TURNER
● NO. OF FOLLOWERS: 359,000 ● NO. OF VIEWS: 54,800,000

ABOUT: Australian TheSimSupply spends a lot of time streaming, but his legacy has been built upon the popularity of his YouTube channel and the diversity of content hosted on it. His videos cover *The Sims* from the first release to the most recent, and you'll even find content for *Sim City*, the city-building game made by the same team as *The Sims*.

HILARIOUSNESS	4
TALKATIVENESS	3
ANGER	2
KNOWLEDGE	3
CREATIVITY	4

ANDREWARCADE

NAME: ANDREW ARCADE
● NO. OF FOLLOWERS: 30,000 ● NO. OF VIEWS: 1,400,000

ABOUT: Although he's more prolific on YouTube, AndrewArcade also streams *The Sims 4* on Twitch, where his funny, sweet, and entertaining personality carries over. He doesn't force his humor, and he doesn't put on a silly voice—you definitely know you're getting someone who is just being himself when streaming, which makes him more fun to watch!

HILARIOUSNESS	4
TALKATIVENESS	3
ANGER	3
KNOWLEDGE	2
CREATIVITY	2

DELIGRACY

NAME: MADELEINE
● NO. OF FOLLOWERS: 270,000 ● NO. OF VIEWS: 47,500,000

ABOUT: Deligracy is one of the most creative Let's Players in *The Sims* community, with lots of tips on how you can build everything from a Barbie-style mansion to the house that looks like a hamburger. As well as a Let's Player and a streamer, she's also a graphic designer, which explains her endless creative ideas and her channel's artsy images.

HILARIOUSNESS	2
TALKATIVENESS	4
ANGER	3
KNOWLEDGE	3
CREATIVITY	4

FROM KOREA TO THE WEST …

BLACK DESERT ONLINE

This MMORPG isn't really *new* in the usual sense. *Black Desert Online* was released in Korea in 2014, but it's only recently made its way to the USA and Europe, which has meant popularity has skyrocketed yet again. There are loads of cool features in *BDO* which make it feel different from other games in the genre, such as the awesome character creator, the ability to climb buildings and obstacles (think *Prince of Persia*!), or the weather system—like how the rain affects your character, making their attacks less powerful. It's no wonder the Twitch community has picked up on the game, from the big-name streamers to MMORPG veterans, all of whom are excited about a new adventure to begin. It's been interesting to see everyone in the United States and Europe learning the game at the same time, and we can't wait to see what secrets they will discover next!

DID YOU KNOW?

There are plenty of Korean games that never get a worldwide release—*MapleStory 2* and *Lost Ark*, for example.

TOP 3 STREAM MOMENTS

BLACK DESERT BEGINS!
SEPTEMBER 26, 2013

1 This is the first day that the MMORPG is shown off, ever, as the Korean media play *Black Desert Online* for a few hours. Excitement builds as the press get excited about the classes, such as Fighter and Sorceress, while the news of a closed beta is announced as well. And thus *Black Desert Online*'s journey begins …

BLACK DESERT IS TOP THREE
OCTOBER 25, 2015

2 *Black Desert Online* managed to crack the top three games on Twitch thanks to the likes of Bikeman and Towelliee all checking out the alpha for the Korean MMORPG ahead of its official release. It even managed to surge ahead of *Dota 2*, and had more viewers than rival Korean game *Blade And Soul*.

BLACK DESERT FOR ALL!
MARCH 3, 2016

3 At last, three years after starting life in Korea, *Black Desert Online* is fully released as a buy-to-play game in the United States and Europe. Curiosity drives initial sales, but word soon spreads about how much fun it is to play, and *Black Desert Online* has now lodged itself in the upper reaches of the Twitch popularity charts.

BIGGEST STREAMERS

WITWIX
NAME: TOM BURKE
- NO. OF FOLLOWERS: **255,000**
- NO. OF VIEWS: **6,800,000**

ABOUT: Knowledgeable and a quick learner, witwix always provides an interesting experience to watch as he blasts his way through games. What we really love is his cool party piece for *Black Desert Online*—when automatically traveling to a new zone, he casually starts whipping through *Super Mario Maker* on the stream in a smaller window. Why not? Dual-wielding games is a trick we'd like to see more often!

HILARIOUSNESS	4
ANGER	2
TALKATIVENESS	3
KNOWLEDGE	5
SKILL	3

KUNGENTV
NAME: UNKNOWN
- NO. OF FOLLOWERS: 220,000 ● NO. OF VIEWS: 69,000,000

ABOUT: If you want to know exactly what makes *Black Desert Online* tick, KungenTV is the man to watch. From canceling animations in combat, to the in-game areas you should be visiting and why, KungenTV has every aspect of *Black Desert Online* covered and explains it all while playing. Even if you consider yourself a veteran, you will learn a new thing or two!

HILARIOUSNESS	1
ANGER	1
TALKATIVENESS	4
KNOWLEDGE	5
SKILL	5

KEYORI
NAME: BARNY BOON
- NO. OF FOLLOWERS: 200,000 ● NO. OF VIEWS: 3,500,000

ABOUT: You know what you're getting with Keyori's streams—a lot of idle chatter, anime soundtracks in the background, and the brightest, most eye-catching T-shirts that you'll ever see! Keyori's streams are great places to hang out, and he's always interacting with his Twitch viewers. If you want to see the game explored at a relaxing pace, this is the place to be.

HILARIOUSNESS	2
ANGER	2
TALKATIVENESS	4
KNOWLEDGE	3
SKILL	2

SCETCHLINK
NAME: UNKNOWN
- NO. OF FOLLOWERS: 10,000 ● NO. OF VIEWS: 125,000

ABOUT: With Scetch's stream, *Black Desert Online* is almost irrelevant. He might be the most talkative person on Twitch, and he talks about everything in life. We don't think he'll ever run out of things to say! He's humble and modest, and slower-paced games like *Black Desert Online* are the perfect choice for him—so you can hear the conversation!

HILARIOUSNESS	1
ANGER	2
TALKATIVENESS	5
KNOWLEDGE	2
SKILL	2

KLERICVEZAX
NAME: UNKNOWN
- NO. OF FOLLOWERS: 5,000 ● NO. OF VIEWS: 171,000

ABOUT: We doubt there's anyone more chilled out on Twitch than KlericVezax. If you just want to see gameplay without being bothered by constant chat, this is the place to be; he just plays through the game at his own pace, enjoying himself as he goes. It's a refreshing change of pace on Twitch and lets you to enjoy *Black Desert Online* without fuss.

HILARIOUSNESS	1
ANGER	0
TALKATIVENESS	1
KNOWLEDGE	2
SKILL	2

BEHIND THE SCENES!

With *Minecraft* music maestro
PHANTABOULOUS

Minecraft singer-songwriter Martijn, known to his fans as Phantaboulous, has over 220,000 YouTube subscribers. Why? Because of his amazing songs, such as his parodies of famous pop songs re-created through *Minecraft*. You've probably seen his fantastic videos. But what is life like on the *other* side of the screen?

MIC CHECK

I treat my microphone like my child. This is the Blue Bluebird, and it really shines on the crispy high frequencies! It hangs in a shock mount, which absorbs all the vibrations from everything else in the room.

LISTENING IN

My Audio Technica headphones. Lovely pair of headphones for accurate representation of my music. What's important is they have a closed design, so the sound doesn't leak back into the mic when I sing!

SPEAK OUT

Studio monitors are very important to represent music as accurately as possible. If it sounds good on these speakers, it sounds good on everything!

AUDIO INTERFACE

My Native Instruments Audio Interface. It amplifies the signal from my microphone and sends it to my computer.

MAJOR KEY

This is my small but functional MIDI keyboard. It's really good for playing melodies, and it also features pads for easier production of drums.

... AND THE END RESULT!

You can see all the equipment Phantaboulous uses here to create his fantastic *Minecraft* parody videos. "Build It All" is a parody of Taylor Swift's "Shake It Off," "The Fights" takes its inspiration from Avicii's "The Nights," and our own favorite "All About That Chase," which is a parody of Meghan Trainor's "All About That Bass." With his biggest videos hitting over 5 million views on YouTube, Phantaboulous is clearly doing something right with his popular parodies!

I'M ALL ABOUT THAT CHASE, GOT THAT

GET FUNKY

I have 13 Funko POP figures right now, from all my favorite movies and series. I think they look really neat on my shelves!

ABSORBING SOUND

This is Auralex foam. It is used to absorb nasty reverb and echo in the room. I thought it was a bit boring, so I turned it into a nice decorative wall!

LEGO MINECRAFT

Of course, *Minecraft* had to be included. It has been such a big part of my life and my YouTube career, I put some figurines with my *Minecraft* skin on there, too!

PLEASE, I'M BEGGING YOU!

GREAT SUCCESS

This is the plaque YouTube sent me when I reached 100,000 subscribers. I'm extremely proud of that, so it's basically on permanent display in my room.

INSPIRING POSTERS

These posters hang behind my screen and remind me that hard work pays off. Sometimes I have a creative block and feel like I'll never finish a song successfully. When I look at the posters I realise that when I do, I'll have the enjoyment of seeing all the nice comments of my fans, which is truly heart-warming and motivating.

READY TO ROCK

I bought this guitar around 10 years ago in standard black and white, but put the red pearl pick guard on there. I love the looks of this Fender Stratocaster!

SOLO TIME

This is my Ibanez from their RG series. While I love my Fender a lot for playing rhythm and chords, my Ibanez really pops when I play guitar solos.

STRUM RIVER

My favorite guitar by far! This is the Taylor GS Mini. What I love about it is that it's a bit smaller than regular acoustic guitars. It's fun to play around with and because of its size, very easy to take on trips.

ON RECORD

These are some random records I bought at a thrift shop, just for decoration. I chose them at random and never listened to them! Some of them have really weird names.

Streamer On ...

FUNNIEST MOMENTS

Who?	Real Name?	Fanbase
Phantaboulous	Martijn	226,000 YouTube subscribers

"For me, being creative means trying new things and exploring possibilities. As a singer, this sometimes means pushing my boundaries a bit. Once when I was recording a parody, I had trouble reaching some high notes. I kept trying and trying, but my voice just could not handle it; it kept breaking and all I got were awful sounds that probably attracted some dogs in the neighborhood ... Anyway, I think I tried for about two hours. Then the doorbell rang. It was the neighbors; they heard someone in distress and wanted to see if everyone was all right. Telling them that the sounds they heard were actually of me singing was a very awkward moment ... "

"All I got were awful sounds that probably attracted some dogs"

GAMING VLOG

BINGO!

Spend enough time watching—or recording!—YouTube videos
and you'll soon notice patterns emerge. Try playing this when
watching someone's videos, or perhaps even one of your own!

GAMING VLOG BINGO!

NUMB3R5 R3PL4CING L3TT3R5 1N Y0UTUB3 U53RN4M3	OPENS WITH A TRADEMARK CATCHPRASE	FANCY INTRO THAT LASTS MORE THAN FIVE SECONDS	READING ON-SCREEN TEXT OUT LOUD
ANNOTATIONS TO CORRECT MISTAKES MADE IN THE VIDEO	ANNOTATIONS THAT LINK TO OTHER VIDEOS	QUICK CUTS TO EDIT TOGETHER ALL THE TALKING	MAKING EXCUSES FOR GETTING LOST IN THE GAME
OVER-THE-TOP REACTION TO ANY SCARE	GUEST APPEARANCE FROM FRIEND	"NONONO NONO NO NOOOOOO!"	LIFE UPDATE VIDEOS WITHOUT ANY GAMEPLAY
PULLING AN AWKWARD FACE IN THE VIDEO THUMBNAIL	REFERRING TO POPULAR MEME	STANDING STILL IN-GAME FOR 15 SECONDS WHILE LAUGHING	"PLEASE COMMENT, LIKE, SUBSCRIBE"

STREAMING FROM THE HOUSE OF THE GODS

SMITE

L aunched in 2013, multiplayer arena brawler *SMITE: Battleground of the Gods* has gone from PC obscurity to one of the most popular titles on the streaming and eSports scenes. It's snapping at the heels of big eSports titles such as *League of Legends* and *Dota 2*, its full-3D action stylings offering a greater spectacle than those titles can provide without losing the tactical depth that has made MOBAs such a hit on Twitch.

It's not just continuing to make waves on the Twitch scene either—*SMITE* has become a mainstay on the pro and semi-pro side of things. In 2015, the game's creator, Hi-Rez Studios, organized the first *SMITE* World Championship. Teams from across the world—including China, Europe, and South America—traveled to Atlanta and competed for an incredible prize fund worth $2.6 million!

DID YOU KNOW?

The second annual *SMITE* World Championship in January 2016 had a prize fund capped at a cool $1,000,000.

TOP 3 STREAM MOMENTS

YAMMYN GETS AN ICY TRIPLE KILL
JANUARY 9, 2016

1 Day three of the *SMITE* World Championships 2016 sees Team Epsilon take on Cloud9 for a place in the next round. Match five starts like any other, but a rush by Cloud9 sees the team turn the aggression up and Yammyn using Ranged Mage Zeus to nab a triple kill.

SHING'S BACCHUS OWNS THE COMPETITION
APRIL 19, 2013

2 While playing during a Twitch stream, eSports pro player Alexander "Shing" Rosa from the US is using his favorite *SMITE* god, Bacchus. His Bacchus is so strong that even when the US pro breaks down in laughter at a friend's joke, his character barely gets a scratch.

NOWHERE TO GO?
SEPTEMBER 1, 2013

3 Inu_ki is an experienced *SMITE* player, so when he trapped an opponent between two of his team's towers, he thought he was guaranteed a kill. With his health low, he backed off to let his minions do some damage. Unfortunately, the opponent had other ideas, leaping towards Inu_ki and killing him!

BIGGEST LET'S PLAYERS

BARRACCUDDA

NAME: JOHN SALTER
- NO. OF FOLLOWERS: 37,000
- NO. OF VIEWS: 3,460,000

ABOUT: John "BaRRaCCuDDa" Salter is a former *Halo: Reach* pro player, competing in MLG Columbus 2012 for the team Crystal Clear. He lives in Cartersville, Georgia, and now plays *SMITE* full-time for the team Cloud9. He plays the role of a Hunter, and is famous for keeping his head clear and not making silly mistakes in the heat of a battle. For some reason, he doesn't wear shoes when he's playing *SMITE*!

HILARIOUSNESS	3
ANGER	2
TALKATIVENESS	4
KNOWLEDGE	4
SKILL	

WEAK3N

NAME: KURT SCHRAY
- NO. OF FOLLOWERS: 36,000
- NO. OF VIEWS: 5,190,000

ABOUT: Kurt "Weak3n" Schray is a pro gamer who left the starting roster of Team EnVyUs to focus on streaming not long after winning the SMITE World Championship 2016 Xbox One Invitational. Weak3n plays the role of Jungler and likes to use assassin-style gods like Hun Batz to cause chaos at any point during his matches.

HILARIOUSNESS	3
ANGER	2
TALKATIVENESS	3
KNOWLEDGE	
SKILL	4

TYDETYME

NAME: TY CHRISTIAN
- NO. OF FOLLOWERS: 43,000
- NO. OF VIEWS: 7,990,000

ABOUT: Ty "TydeTyme" Christian used to love playing *League of Legends* before switching over to *SMITE*. TydeTyme can sometimes lose his temper in a very amusing way! He has three favorite gods he likes to use that suit his playstyle: the powerful water deity Poseidon is his top choice, followed by the god of music, Apollo and ranged magician He Bo.

HILARIOUSNESS	2
ANGER	1
TALKATIVENESS	3
KNOWLEDGE	4
SKILL	3

SUNTOUCH

NAME: PETER LOGAN
- NO. OF FOLLOWERS: 46,000
- NO. OF VIEWS: 3,000,000

ABOUT: Peter "Suntouch" Logan is a member of top eSports outfit Team Dignitas, so you'd expect him to know *SMITE* well … but his knowledge and skill are outstanding. Although he's not the chattiest streamer and doesn't offer too much insight into what's happening, he's definitely one of the best to watch if you want to see high-level *SMITE* gameplay.

HILARIOUSNESS	2
ANGER	3
TALKATIVENESS	2
KNOWLEDGE	
SKILL	

INCON

NAME: RILEY UNZELMAN
- NO. OF FOLLOWERS: 34,000
- NO. OF VIEWS: 5,970,000

ABOUT: Riley "Incon" Unzelman is an American professional *SMITE* player and YouTuber currently signed to Team Flex. Incon often plays in the Guardian role, providing support for other players by using tougher characters that can soak up damage, which is why he uses Ares and Bacchus. He used to play for the teams AFK Gaming and Team EnVyUs.

HILARIOUSNESS	
ANGER	3
TALKATIVENESS	4
KNOWLEDGE	4
SKILL	

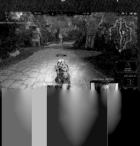

PICKING A GOD HAS NEVER BEEN SO EASY ...

STREAMERS' TOP PICKS

JANUS

STREAMER: MLCST3ALTH
PRIMARY ROLE: Mage
RELIGION: Roman

CORE ITEMS
Spear of Desolation, Rod of Tahuti, Spear of the Magus

ABOUT
Janus is all about using portals—he can create a portal to pass through walls, or to drop enemies from great heights.

ABILITIES

PASSAGES (PASSIVE)

PORTAL

UNSTABLE VORTEX

THRESHOLD

OSIRIS

STREAMER: CycloneSpin
PRIMARY ROLE: Warrior
RELIGION: Egyptian

CORE ITEMS
Rage, Deathbringer, The Executioner

ABOUT
When you want to get a little more physical with an opponent, Osiris is a great choice, thanks to his high-damage abilities ...

ABILITIES

FRAGMENTED (PASSIVE)

SICKLE STRIKE

JUDGEMENT TETHER

SPIRIT FLAIL

STREAMERS' TOP TIPS

FIND THE GOD THAT SUITS YOUR PLAYSTYLE
Some pros might favor a certain character, but that doesn't mean you have to. "I encourage people to do their own thing," says pro Lassiz.

WANT TO GO PRO? PLAY AGAINST THE BEST
"If you want to get into the professional scene, the only way that I know how to do it is to climb the ranked ladder," comments pro player Incon.

GET CONFIDENT & START PLAYING AGGRESSIVE
"My playstyle may develop, such as playing passive when someone's near my wards, but I'll mostly play aggressive," says eSports pro Shing.

PRACTICE A LOT AND STUDY YOUR OPPONENTS
Studying what your foes are doing is important. "You have to know your opponent better than they know themselves," advises pro MLCom3ga.

THANATOS

STREAMER: Frostiak
PRIMARY ROLE: Assassin
RELIGION: Greek

CORE ITEMS
Hydra's Lament, Brawler's Beat Stick, Titan's Bane

ABOUT
In Greek mythology, Thanatos is the face of death. In *SMITE*, he's a fearsome assassin who can take down enemies fast.

ABILITIES

SCENT OF DEATH

SOUL REAP

HARVESTER OF SOULS (PASSIVE)

DEATH SCYTHE

CUPID

STREAMER: Snakeskin
PRIMARY ROLE: Hunter
RELIGION: Roman

CORE ITEMS
Ichaival, Rage, Deathbringer

ABOUT
This lovable little guy is much more dangerous than he looks. His arrows do a lot of damage, and he can heal his teammates—a useful skill.

ABILITIES

LOVESTRUCK (PASSIVE)

HEART BOMB

SHARE THE LOVE

FLUTTER

YMIR

STREAMER: CaptainTwig
PRIMARY ROLE: Guardian
RELIGION: Norse

CORE ITEMS
Soul Reaver, Gem of Isolation, Void Stone

ABOUT
The king of the Nordic Frost Giants is a terrifying creature, not only because of his appearance, but because of his freezing skills.

ABILITIES

FROSTBITE (PASSIVE)

ICE WALL

GLACIAL STRIKE

FROST BREATH

PRO INTERVIEW

KIWI TIGER

We hear about Kiwi Tiger's rise to pro status in the eSports scene and what new players should do to succeed.

First, tell us a little about how you got into the eSports scene?

I first started getting into the *SMITE* eSports scene around May 2014. When I felt I was ready to start getting into more competitive gaming as a Solo Laner; I jumped from team to team for a while, even swapping roles to Support until I decided to try and make my own team.

Of all the MOBAs to choose from, why settle on *SMITE*?

I had looked at other MOBAs, such as *Dota 2* and *League of Legends*, but the top-down perspective always discouraged me from playing because it seemed like it didn't require much skill and that it would be boring just clicking around the map. *SMITE*, however, is third-person, and most of the abilities in *SMITE* require you to aim, so you feel more in control.

SMITE allows for individual flair and creativity, but it's still very much a team-orientated experience—how crucial is that sense of cooperation and communication?

It's really critical to any *SMITE* team as you can't win a game alone. Knowing when the enemy is missing from a lane or when a critical ability is down can help keep your team safe or turn a fight around. Even just knowing that most of the enemy is on one side of the map can give your team the advantage to get an objective or push down a tower.

Do you have a Twitch or YouTube account? If so, how have these platforms helped you develop as a pro?

I have both a Twitch and a YouTube account. I mainly use them to watch higher players play and see what they do so I can improve my own skills.

What advice would you offer someone looking to take their *SMITE* skills into the competitive scene? How can they prepare for such a transition?

Such a transition can be a big step but no-one should be scared to take it. The first thing is to know the role that fits your playstyle. You don't want to choose a role you find boring or frustrating. After choosing a role, know the gods in your class. There may be some gods you simply don't like or they don't fit how you play, but you should know quite a few gods in your role so you can play what your team needs.

A ROLE-PLAYING CLASSIC
RUNESCAPE

The MMORPG is the genre with the most staying power. No other genre offers the thrilling journey towards building a dominant character through unlocking skills and discovering powerful new gear to use. When it comes to staying power, *RuneScape* is the grand master of all MMORPGs having lasted over 15 years thanks to its intricate skill system, expansive quests, and vast game world. It's become so

popular, it has even had its own annual *RuneFest* expo in London since 2010.

There are a few variations available, from *Old School RuneScape* that plays just as it was originally released, all the way up to the current look seen on these pages. Whichever style you prefer, the frequent free updates and vibrant community will ensure this long-standing RPG grows into the modern age.

DID YOU KNOW?
If you want *Old School RuneScape* without downloading it, you can stream the classic RPG in any web browser.

TOP 3 LET'S PLAY MOMENTS

THE FALADOR INCIDENT
JUNE 7, 2006

1 A glitch caused indirectly by a new skill led to accidental mayhem. The first user to reach level 99 in the skill hosted a party at his in-game house, and some attendees decided to engage in PvP. But then they kept their PvP status in the main world, and the Purge-like chaos cost victims over 2 billion coins.

THE LONE VICTOR
NOVEMBER 1, 2015

2 A lone wanderer in *Old School RuneScape* ventured alone into a hostile desert, looking for a certain enemy holding a huge sum of loot. After finding his prey he attacked, eventually killing him and claiming the treasure. This sounds ordinary, but the epic soundtrack made the kill seem more amazing than it actually was.

LUCKIEST RUNESCAPE MOMENT EVER?
NOVEMBER 21, 2012

3 Long-time YouTube *RuneScape* player B0aty was grinding a dungeon when he came across a Dust Devil enemy. Having killed thousands of them before, he thought nothing of it and slayed him, only to receive an incredibly rare piece of armor. His shocked reaction is hilarious.

BIGGEST STREAMERS

MMORPGRS
NAME: CURTIS
- NO. OF FOLLOWERS: 73,000
- NO. OF VIEWS: 2,400,000

ABOUT: Curtis, aka "MmorpgRS," has been playing *RuneScape* for about ten years, first signing up around Easter 2007. Since then he's become one of the top *RuneScape* streamers, racking up over 70,000 followers. He regularly takes on in-game Iron Man challenges to test his strengths, making him a great watch for anyone who wants to see the most difficult parts of a game.

HILARIOUSNESS	3
TALKATIVENESS	3
ANGER	2
KNOWLEDGE	5
SKILL	5

MR_MAMMAL
NAME: JORDAN
- NO. OF FOLLOWERS: 71,000 ● NO. OF VIEWS: 1,800,000

ABOUT: Mr_Mammal is one of the youngest streamers on Twitch, but he has built quite a following for himself playing *Old School RuneScape*. He's been making videos for YouTube since he was only 12 years old, so he knows his way around a camera and it shows. He's a pretty good *RuneScape* player, too, so he's worth a look.

HILARIOUSNESS	3
TALKATIVENESS	4
ANGER	1
KNOWLEDGE	3
SKILL	4

FATNOOBLET
NAME: N/A
- NO. OF FOLLOWERS: 15,000 ● NO. OF VIEWS: 300,000

ABOUT: Having played *RuneScape* since 2006, FatNooblet has a vast amount of knowledge and experience to call upon for his YouTube videos. He puts together videos that showcase all aspects of *RuneScape* and offers tips on how to attack enemies, what builds he uses and other tricks to help improve your gameplay.

HILARIOUSNESS	4
TALKATIVENESS	4
ANGER	1
KNOWLEDGE	5
SKILL	5

SABER_SIX
NAME: ERIN
- NO. OF FOLLOWERS: 24,000 ● NO. OF VIEWS: 810,000

ABOUT: Saber_Six is a longtime *RuneScape* player and streamer, first playing the game in 2004 and streaming her exploits in September 2012. Her total level of 1695 in *Old School RuneScape*, and 2426 in the modern version, is a testament to how much time she's put into the game. Her musical parodies add a fun element to her streams, too.

HILARIOUSNESS	3
TALKATIVENESS	4
ANGER	2
KNOWLEDGE	5
SKILL	3

GRAPHISTRS
NAME: BRANDON
- NO. OF FOLLOWERS: 22,000 ● NO. OF VIEWS: 360,000

ABOUT: GraphistRS calls himself an "old-school PKer," which means he's a PvP player in *Old School RuneScape*. His stream purely involves entering the game, turning on PvP, and fighting as many other players as he can for loot. Other channels might feature exploration or dungeons, but GraphistRS is the guy for pure PvP combat and a cool soundtrack.

HILARIOUSNESS	3
TALKATIVENESS	3
ANGER	4
KNOWLEDGE	5
SKILL	3

NEWEST GAME ON THE BLOCK

OVERWATCH

Blizzard Entertainment has created some of the most successful franchises in video-game history, with big hitters like *World of Warcraft* and *Hearthstone* being two of the most notable. So when the company decides to announce a brand new franchise, the industry takes notice. When *Overwatch* debuted at BlizzCon 2014, the cartoon-style graphics were so amazing that viewers at first thought they were watching a Pixar movie trailer instead of the next great Blizzard game! They soon realized that what they were actually looking at was a fast and frenetic multiplayer first-person shooter that takes inspiration from the MOBA genre in offering a diverse roster of colorful characters with unique abilities to play as. *Overwatch* is all about capturing and defending objectives, so teamwork is just as important as your shooting skills.

DID YOU KNOW?
There are four combat types in *Overwatch* that you can use: offensive, defensive, tank, and support.

TOP 3 STREAM MOMENTS

"I BELIEVE!"
OCTOBER 28, 2015

1 A Winston player was on the attack with his team, with the other team holed with shields protecting every one of the players. Winston used his super-jump to leap quickly over the shields and behind the enemy team, before unloading his weapon and taking them out before they realised what was happening.

COOL GIRLS DON'T LOOK AT EXPLOSIONS
NOVEMBER 27, 2015

2 In one of the funniest moments you'll ever see in *Overwatch*, a player using D.Va sent her self-destructing mech into a crowd of enemies, turned her back to the scene, and then watched the kills rack up after taking out five of the six players on the opposing team.

FLICK OF THE WRIST
DECEMBER 19, 2015

3 A talented Hanzo player amazed viewers by scoring one-hit kills on all six opposing team members while using only seven arrows. He starts by taking out three of the six on a rooftop as they pass by, then quickly descends to the ground and eliminates the other three. If this were *Lord Of The Rings*, this guy would be Legolas.

BIGGEST LET'S PLAYERS

TIMTHETATMAN
NAME: TIM
- NO. OF FOLLOWERS: 70,000
- NO. OF VIEWS: 23,500,000

ABOUT: 25-year-old Tim the Tat Man (can you guess why that's his name?) is a full-time Let's Player with a speciality in shooters and fast-paced games. Its not surprising, then, that his newest darling is *Overwatch*, and he has been streaming every single one of his online matches. He will occasionally throw in an RPG or adventure game on his channel, but first-person shooters are his mainstay.

HILARIOUSNESS	4
TALKATIVENESS	4
ANGER	3
KNOWLEDGE	3
SKILL	5

FAIRLIGHT EXCALIBUR
NAME: JESSE
- NO. OF FOLLOWERS: 12,000 ● NO. OF VIEWS: 140,000

ABOUT: Known for his marathon streams across a variety of games, Jesse is a big fan of *Overwatch*. He maintains a high level of play despite playing for an exhausting amount of hours, always able to analyze the action and break down team compositions, opponent play styles and his character strengths during the match.

HILARIOUSNESS	3
TALKATIVENESS	4
ANGER	2
KNOWLEDGE	5
SKILL	5

YUUIE
NAME: NATALIE
- NO. OF FOLLOWERS: 8,000 ● NO. OF VIEWS: 400,000

ABOUT: Yuuie's is one of the best *Overwatch* players on YouTube (and an occasional cosplayer). She plays a lot of different games, particularly those with anime origins and inspirations, but when it's time to pick up a gun and display some action skills, she's certainly no slouch. Her cheerful nature makes her Let's Plays a lot of fun to experience.

HILARIOUSNESS	4
TALKATIVENESS	5
ANGER	1
KNOWLEDGE	4
SKILL	4

POKELAWLS
NAME: UNKNOWN
- NO. OF FOLLOWERS: 5,000 ● NO. OF VIEWS: 2,400,000

ABOUT: His name might make you think he's a Pokémon master, but Pokelawls has much more in his repertoire. The Canadian plays all kinds of games on his channel, but recently he's been honing his skills as the agile character Genji. His real name is unknown, but Pokelawls is a name to remember when looking for a Let's Play or stream.

HILARIOUSNESS	3
TALKATIVENESS	2
ANGER	3
KNOWLEDGE	4
SKILL	4

A_SEAGULL
NAME: BRANDON LARNED
- NO. OF FOLLOWERS: 6,000 ● NO. OF VIEWS: 310,000

ABOUT: For competitive *Overwatch*, watch A_Seagull. As a member of Luminosity.gg's eSports team, Brandon knows every in and out of *Overwatch*, and showcases Blizzard's shooter at a very high level of play. From hopeless newcomers to savvy veterans, anyone looking to gain an edge in *Overwatch* should check out his channel.

HILARIOUSNESS	1
TALKATIVENESS	1
ANGER	3
KNOWLEDGE	4
SKILL	5

STAT ATTACK

Over **100** mph max possible speed

17 Million+ sales to date

Life: 400/400   Mana

TERRARIA

Thanks to its clever mix of exploration, adventure, building and combat, *Terraria* was an instant hit as soon as it was released. Just nine days after it went on sale in May 2011, it already had over 200,000 sales, and within the first month, it sold over 432,000 copies. Four years later and several huge updates later, it's still going strong!

Over
3,000
items including
weapons and
armor

50,000+
players a
week

THE BIGGEST YOUTUBE & GAMING CONVENTIONS IN THE WORLD!

E3

This is the biggest gaming event around, bar none! It's where gaming publishers, including the very biggest like Sony, Microsoft, and Nintendo, show off their upcoming games and hardware for the first time. Sadly, E3 isn't open to the public. However YouTubers and Twitch streamers may be invited to attend, so there's no place to find a bigger collection of gaming celebrities! If you're super-interested, and live near Los Angeles, it's worth checking to see if there are any YouTube and Twitch meet-ups happening around E3 time.

Forza Horizon 3 brings the game series to Australia, complete with kangaroos!

LEGENDS OF GAMING

The biggest names in gaming descend on London for the explosive Legends of Gaming event, which features the likes of TheDiamondMinecart, AshleyMariee and Calfreezy. What makes this particular expo unique is that you get to see them playing each other at different games like *FIFA*, *Minecraft*, *Mario Kart* and *Tekken*. A final score is tallied and the overall Legend of Gaming is crowned!

An all-new *Spider-Man* game was announced at E3 2016 for PlayStation 4

INSOMNIA

Alhough Insomnia began life as a gaming competition, it has now grown to include so much more than that—it has cosplay, a bring-your-own-console area, a Tabletop Zone for board game fans, and even its very own Minecraft Zone! The prestige of the event means bigger YouTube stars also attend—previous attendees include NettyPlays, AmyLee33 and Gizzy Gazza!

TWITCHCON

The "official" Twitch convention, this event sees the biggest and best Twitch broadcasters in the world unite under one roof. Everyone who's anyone in the world of Twitch goes to Twitchcon—previous names include the likes of KittyPlaysGames, imaqtpie, Lethalfrag, Ms_Vixen, Maximilian_DOOD, IAmSp00n, CaptainSparklez and SethBling! It goes without saying that anyone who wants to learn from the best should watch Twitchcon when it's streamed live through—where else?—Twitch.

PAX

With four events in the United States and one in Australia as well, Penny Arcade Expo (PAX for short) is the gaming culture event that covers everything you can think of and more. Interviews with the biggest developers, live music performances, mystery tournaments, cosplay, cool indie games, career workshops … there's so much happening at PAX that it's hard to fit everything in! Of course, there are also the YouTube stars— Captain Sparklez, Game Grumps, and Markiplier have all showed up at the event in recent years.

STREAMCON

Proving that it's not just the West Coast that has all the fun, StreamCon is New York's very own celebration of all things video! Focusing on YouTube, names take part across all spectrums of YouTube, from entertainment to comedy to music—gaming fans will recognize names like Catrific and iJustine. Even better, because StreamCon usually takes place around Halloween, there are special Halloween events, such as a Halloween concert and Halloween costume contest!

© Vincent Samaco

BLIZZCON

This massive two-day event is a celebration of all things Blizzard, perfect for fans of *World of Warcraft*, *Hearthstone*, *StarCraft II*, and *Overwatch*! This is where Blizzard makes huge announcements about its games and hosts high-level tournaments showcasing the best players in the world. And, of course, famous YouTubers and Twitch streamers known for their Blizzard expertise cover all the action.

GAMESCOM

While it's not quite as big as E3, Gamescom is still the biggest gaming event in Europe, and even better, it's open to the public! Dominated by four massive gaming halls, there are all sorts of exciting things happening—game announcements, huge competitions, exciting tournaments and, of course, big name YouTubers and streamers there in person. You'll live Gamescom through their eyes as they cover the action from the public displays to sneaky peeks behind closed doors at new games.

SUMMER IN THE CITY

With talks, panels and live performances, London's Summer in the City is the biggest YouTube event around! Because it's not just dedicated to gamers on YouTube, the size of the event means YouTube heroes like Amazing Phil and Hazel Hayes mingle alongside your favorite gaming legends. Anyone looking for expert advice to boost their YouTube profile should definitely keep an eye on the videos that come out after the event—hearing the best in the world offer their advice and experience is priceless.

VIDCON

This huge three-day event is dedicated to all aspects of online video, so YouTube and Twitch fans will feel right at home, including those who are also on Vine! It takes place at the massive Anaheim Center in California, and there's a special focus on workshops to help video creators sharpen their skills, so it's definitely an event that's worth watching on YouTube or Twitch.

Photographer: Curious-Josh

SPAMFISH

FROM OVERWATCH TO MARIO, SPAMFISH DOES IT ALL!

Entertaining someone to make them laugh, smile, or have fun is a sincerely profound gift.

STARTING OUT

What made you start streaming?

● I started watching streams on Justin.tv. I loved the ability to be part of someone's else gameplay experience and watching people play. After about three years of watching, I was able to give streaming a go after getting a decent PC. I wanted to be part of what was some of the most engaging content I'd ever seen, and this was back when gaming on Justin.tv was a section of a larger livestreaming site with lifecams, science, movies, and more. I wanted to share my passion for games and for ranting my deluded opinions at the world.

What was the toughest part to overcome?

● The toughest thing was the technical side, having stable Internet, efficiency of using streaming programs, testing settings, and being prepared for unforeseen issues. I'm still trying to overcome the evil tech gremlins today! One of the hardest things is simple discovery, people having the chance to see your content.

When I started streaming, there were maybe a few hundred livestreams at any time, and anyone with over 100 viewers was a *huge* channel. Now there are sometimes over 30,000 streams live at any one time, with the biggest streamers getting tens of thousands of viewers.

Was there a moment when you thought "wow, I've made it!"?

I guess when I was hosting coverage for Twitch at E3 last year, interviewing Tony Hawk with thousands of people watching, there was a sense of, "Wow. What is my life?!"

THE GAMES

What is the Mariothon and what made you decide to do it?

● The Mariothon is all the main system *Mario* games being played to 100 percent completion. I have always struggled with organization and structure, and have always been a huge Nintendo fanboy, so I thought it would be a good way of becoming more professional whilst also celebrating my love for the series of games, while also exploring how the games and mechanics have developed over the years. Organization and consistency are two huge factors for any successful streamer, and this was a natural way of growing my stream whilst also having fun and achieving lifelong gamer goals.

What games have worked out better than you thought they would when you're streaming?

● Playing a very small and unique indie game called *Papers, Please* remains my most hyped, talked-about, and watched casts of alltime. Even though I only played it for a few hours, people still ask me to play it again almost every day and remember it fondly. Conversely, despite loving sports games, they are quite divisive.

What's been your all-time favorite streaming moment?

● Well it isn't my favorite, but the "motherlode" [Spamfish made an embarrassing mistake in *Fallout 4*] is probably my most infamous moment while streaming. But the great thing about streaming is that there are incredible moments every day.

STREAMING

What's the coolest thing about being a streamer?

● Being able to share something I'm really passionate about with people around the world and being able to be there for someone when they are having a bad day. Entertaining someone to make them laugh, smile, or have fun is a sincerely profound gift that streaming gives, both from watching and streaming! Also the free games, haha!

What are the downsides of being a streamer?

● It can be mentally draining and also very competitive. From a job perspective, you can't really afford to take any time off from streaming without stopping growing. You do end up spending lots of time on your own in front of a screen, often sacrificing real-life interactions, friends and family, and fearing the Sun! There is also the issue of playing games off-stream; sometimes you might want to play a game for yourself but feel you should share it with your community.

How often do you watch other streams?

● Everyday. I've been watching streams for far longer than I have been streaming myself. I watch streams all the time, it is by far one of my favorite things to do! I will always consider myself more of a viewer than a caster.

Watch out! Over there!
Spamfish playing Overwatch

Video Description
The broadcaster has not set a description for this video

QUICKFIRE

If you could change Spamfish to any other username, what would you change it to?

● Before I started streaming, I was thinking of changing my name, as having the name Spamfish meant people thought I was a 12-year-old troll and would often get banned in channels simply for my name. I was actually giving consideration to changing it to "ThePeopleWhoCareDont" just before I started streaming. So, so bad and glad I didn't change!

What are your hobbies outside of gaming?

● I love watching sports, particularly soccer and the NFL. I'm also a big fan of movies and TV as well.

What's your favorite Twitch emote?

● Probably KappaHD. It's an even more smug version of Kappa.

What's your worst habit?

● Eating sweet things. Mental capitulation.

NOT A CREEPER IN SIGHT

STARCRAFT

The *StarCraft* series is not just a fan favorite in the eSports world, it's also one of the biggest real-time strategy titles around.

The game gives you command of an entire army of soldiers in a space-age world, and your only mission is to fight back against the oncoming swarms of enemies. There are three races to choose from—the human-like Terran, the blue, floating Protoss and the terrifying, monstrous Zerg. You can command whole groups of your troops or individual units, and managing your army (including gathering resources and defending your base) is just as important as taking the enemy down.

In eSports circles, *StarCraft* is known as one of the toughest games in which to compete. Its focus on strategy also makes *StarCraft* one of the most psychologically grueling eSports that you can compete in. The level of concentration required when facing off against the best players in the world is tougher than many people realize. This makes it great to watch—but it's also fun to play at home, if you think you can handle the pressure.

DID YOU KNOW?
StarCraft is so popular in Korea that even the air force has its own competitive eSports team, called Air Force ACE.

TOP 3 ESPORTS MOMENTS

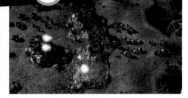

WHEN A GOOD PLAN BACKFIRES
NOVEMBER 6, 2015

1 When Hydra took on Rogue at the *StarCraft 2* World Championship Series, his plan was simple: Zerg rush his way into Rogue's base and lay waste to anything that moves. While a good strategy, it wasn't Hydra's day. Rogue crippled Hydra's armada after just four minutes.

THE ULTIMATE UNDERDOG
OCTOBER 7, 2011

2 A relative unknown, Lee "PuMa" Ho Joon, once decided to enter the NASL Open. After qualifying for the final's live event, PuMa went on to defeat fan favorites and even "July," a *StarCraft: Brood War* legend, in the fourth round. After that, only the legendary Jang "MC" Min Chul stood in PuMa's way. Amazingly, PuMa won!

WATCH YOUR STEP
APRIL 2, 2015

3 Two games down against Kim "Soulkey" Min Chul at the *SSL Season 2* tournament, Kim "Cure" Doh Wook was seconds away from losing, so in a last-ditch attempt to steal a win, he led an assault. But Soulkey had laid down two Baneling landmines. In a split second, some 30 Marines were eliminated all at once.

BIGGEST STREAMERS

TLO

NAME: Dario Wünsch
- **NO. OF FOLLOWERS:** 62,000
- **NO. OF VIEWS:** 26,000,000

ABOUT: TLO plays for Team Liquid—one of the most prolific teams out there—and is known for his always cheerful personality. Although TLO plays as the Zerg race, it wasn't always like that. Starting out, he'd always select Random—a tactic seldom used in the competitive scene—but moved on to Terran before eventually rolling Zerg. Many believe TLO's greatest strength is the ability to create innovative strategies that no opponent sees coming.

HILARIOUSNESS	4
ANGER	2
TALKATIVENESS	5
GAME KNOWLEDGE	5
SKILL	4

WINTERGAMING

NAME: EVAN BALLNIK
- NO. OF FOLLOWERS: 114,000 ● NO. OF VIEWS: 9,500,000

ABOUT: Winter is a Random player, which means he allows the game to select a race for him at the start of each match, since he is adept at all three. His streams are friendly, welcoming and educational for all players. Winter has raised his highest rank to Grand Master both as a Zerg player and a Random player—which means he's *very* good.

GAME KNOWLEDGE	4
FRIENDLINESS	5
SKILL	3
ANGER	1
CRAFTING SKILLS	3

EGHUK

NAME: CHRIS LORANGER
- NO. OF FOLLOWERS: 48,000 ● NO. OF VIEWS: 16,800,000

ABOUT: Known for his unpredictable playing style, HuK loves to keep his opponents guessing. His appreciation for his fans led to them giving him nicknames including "HuK Norris" and "The Incredible HuK." His achievements are plentiful, having won HomeStory Cup 3, LANHAMMER 2013, SHOUTcraft America Winter, and he's often in the top five.

GAME KNOWLEDGE	5
FRIENDLINESS	3
SKILL	3
ANGER	4
CRAFTING SKILLS	3

SCARLETTM

NAME: SASHA HOSTYN
- NO. OF FOLLOWERS: 14,034 ● NO. OF VIEWS: 665,593

ABOUT: Scarlett is known for her Zerglings, Banelings, Mutalisks, and more importantly, her Creep spread and strategies. She's won four major tournaments, and she's one of only three women to win a pro *StarCraft* match on Korean TV. She dislikes the Protoss race, and has said that she would redesign them from scratch if she could.

GAME KNOWLEDGE	3
FRIENDLINESS	1
SKILL	3
ANGER	4
CRAFTING SKILLS	5

HERO

NAME: SONG HYEON DEOK
- NO. OF FOLLOWERS: 29,707 ● NO. OF VIEWS: 8,406,036

ABOUT: HerO started playing *StarCraft* at just 15. Since then, the former Team Liquid member has become one of the most decorated players in Korea, winning several tournaments. As a fan of Warp Prism, in a match against Life he used his ability in conjunction with Immortal. This unexpected combo ended up raking in a whopping 40 kills.

GAME KNOWLEDGE	5
FRIENDLINESS	3
SKILL	3
ANGER	5
CRAFTING SKILLS	4

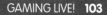

HOW TO UP YOUR GAME AND COMPETE WITH THE PROS

STARCRAFT 2 TOP TIPS

TAKE CARE OF NUMBER ONE

Sometimes, *StarCraft* matches can be so fun and so engaging that you can lose track of time. Remember to take regular breaks—the game requires real focus, which is impossible if you don't take a timeout.

PREPARE TO PROBE

The Protoss race has access to a construction unit known as a Probe. Probes are a blessing if you need to see what the enemy's up to. Plus, harassing Terran Barracks is a great way to slow them down.

TOP 3 PRO PLAYERS' TOP PICKS

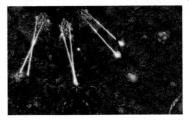

PROTOSS
PLAYER NAME ShoWTimE
CAME IN FIRST IN THE ESL MEISTERSCHAFT GERMANY: WINTER SEASON 2015

The Protoss race is known for its aggressive tactics and the ability to teleport large numbers of units into enemy territory. Units also have a plasma shield, which speeds up regeneration after combat.

ZERG
PLAYER NAME Serral
PLACED FIRST IN ASSEMBLY WINTER 2016

Speed is the Zerg race's forte. Upgraded Zerglings can zip around the map at a blinding speed, and Roaches and Infesters can move around while burrowed. Though the Zerg are considered the hardest race to engage in combat with, they're a formidable force.

TERRAN
PLAYER NAME INnoVation
WON THE 2015 GLOBAL STARCRAFT 2 LEAGUE SEASON THREE

Nicknamed the "easy" race, Terrans are known for their defenses. The goal for most is to build a heavily fortified position quickly. They don't launch an assault until they're ready, and can remain unchallenged while they're building their forces.

THERE'S NO POINT BEING RICH

Minerals are important, but simply amassing a fortune is pointless if you don't use them. You should never have over 1,000 minerals; there is always something it could be spent on.

USE THOSE HOTKEYS

Hotkeys are there for a reason: to provide a quicker way to jump between units. Learning how to use them will make a big difference in your game. A few seconds here and there might not sound like much, but it all adds up.

KNOW YOUR ENEMIES

Mastering the race that works for you is important, but being aware of the potential threats is equally as important. Who are they? What can they do to your defenses? Where are they? Always be aware of—and question—who it is you're fighting.

THE INTERNET

If in doubt, look online. Never be afraid to type the words "[Race name] + Beginner Build" into your favorite search engine. Everyone starts out as a newbie, or "noob," so get online, and start reading guides to help bolster your tactics.

LOSING IS GOOD

No-one wants to lose, but when you're starting out, it's going to happen. Don't be discouraged, though. Every loss is a chance to figure out what it is you're doing wrong, and therefore how to fix it and improve.

PRO INTERVIEW

DARIO "TLO" WUNSCH

As one of the strongest players in Europe, Dario "TLO" Wünsch has gone toe to toe with the best of the best players in the StarCraft world.

What has been your biggest accomplishment to date?
Reaching the semifinals at IEM São Paulo has been my deepest run in a major SC2 tournament so far.

How many hours do you have to put in when training for an event?
If I'm training for a really important tournament, I try to train six to nine hours a day, every day, with a maximum of one free day a week for an entire month leading up to the event. Usually, I attend big events every one or two months.

In 2015, Blizzard introduced a rule where players need to have residential status to play in tournaments. What are your thoughts on this?
Well I do believe it helps the scene overall to [get] more diversity and fan interest, but I do hope we'll eventually get a good amount of global events so we can still keep competing with South Koreans. It's exciting to play against the best of the best.

In South Korea, there's a huge amount of money in the eSports scene. Can European countries and the United States reach a similar level?
I don't [see] why not. South Korea's big advantage was that the [eSports] scene happened in one city. Logistics helped grow the level of professionalism faster. But as eSports is attracting more money, those logistical problems become less of an issue. I believe eSports in Europe and the United States is overtaking South Korea in many regards already.

If you could give advice to people looking to get into playing competitively as a full-time job, what would it be?
If you're working towards something as unlikely as becoming a pro gamer, it's important that you don't just try to become a better gamer, but to become a more capable and confident person. It's likely you won't end up with your dream career so it's important that you'll be happy with the time invested towards your goals even if it doesn't work out. If you give it your all, the skills you acquired will help you no matter what you'll end up doing in life.

INDIE GEM SCORES A WINNER

ROCKET LEAGUE

Rocket League has only been out since July 2015 and it's already one of the biggest games on Twitch. It's also got a pretty impressive following on YouTube, with everyone from sports fans to pro gamers posting videos showing off the rockets-meets-cars-meets-soccer combo. Its popularity with gamers and the media has propelled it into superstar status, and it remains consistently in the top ten games on Twitch.

Twitch has played a huge part in *Rocket League*'s rise into the world of eSports. The Electronics Sports League (ESL) now has professional tournaments in both Europe and North America, and the simple rules of the game—a team of three RC-style cars need to push or boost a giant metal ball into their opponent's goal—has made it a perfect game to sit back, watch, and enjoy.

DID YOU KNOW?

In December 2015, a team of YouTubers was awarded a Guinness World Record for the Most Goals in One Match—a crazy 41!

STREAMERS' TOP TIPS

DON'T BE A SCAREDY-CAT KEEPER

"Defending aggressively—something I'm starting to learn—is important. You still want to be first to the ball and chasing the ball down when you're on defense," advises pro Coolcole.

GET YOUR AIM RIGHT WHEN BOOSTING

"You need to be able to get into a proper trajectory early in your flight, so you can use the extra time you have to aim the shot," says pro Fyshokid of aerial shots.

REMEMBER YOUR POSITIONING

Don't be fooled into rushing for the ball. "It all comes down to positioning," says Team Rocket member Doomsee. "Always be aware of where you are, and where others are, on the field."

DON'T FORGET ABOUT DEFENDING

If you're playing with players you don't know, always defend as a default, since most players rush off. "I usually try to be a bit defensive, just to see how it plays out," says Fyshokid.

BIGGEST LET'S PLAYERS

VIRTUAL TRIDENT
NAME: TIM
- NO. OF FOLLOWERS: 5,700
- NO. OF VIEWS: 45,000

ABOUT: Virtual Trident's channel strikes the perfect balance between showcasing skill, dedication, and a friendly community atmosphere. His channel proves it is every bit as much fun to watch *Rocket League* as it is to actually play it yourself … plus you can learn a trick or two just by watching him play!

HILARIOUSNESS	1
TALKATIVENESS	2
ANGER	2
KNOWLEDGE	4
SKILL	4

CAMGEARS
NAME: CAMERON BILLS
- NO. OF FOLLOWERS: 99,000
- NO. OF VIEWS: 690,000

ABOUT: Cameron Bills, aka CamGears/Kronovi, is one of the longest-serving players in the *Rocket League* community, having played its prequel (*Supersonic Acrobatic Rocket-Powered Battle-Cars*) for six years before *Rocket League* arrived. He plays *Rocket League* regularly and even played professionally at one point.

HILARIOUSNESS	2
TALKATIVENESS	4
ANGER	2
KNOWLEDGE	4
SKILL	3

GIBBS0O0
NAME: RANDY GIBBONS
- NO. OF FOLLOWERS: 33,000
- NO. OF VIEWS: 5,700,000

ABOUT: Let's Player and streamer Randy "Gibbs0o0" Gibbons lives in the United States, and has become one of *Rocket League*'s most popular players. He formed a team known as Cosmic Aftershock with Kronovi and SadJunior. SadJunior has left the team, but Gambit and Lachinio have since joined, and the group is now the top outfit in North America.

HILARIOUSNESS	3
TALKATIVENESS	4
ANGER	2
KNOWLEDGE	4
SKILL	4

N0IR1992
NAME: BIRK
- NO. OF FOLLOWERS: 5,000
- NO. OF VIEWS: 53,000

ABOUT: German *Rocket League* player N0ir_1992 knows how to have a good time while playing *Rocket League*, and as a result, his channel is relaxing and laid-back, especially given how competitive the game can get! He streams in English, and he's a good player too, so you'll pick up plenty of tips while watching the 23-year-old play.

HILARIOUSNESS	3
TALKATIVENESS	4
ANGER	4
KNOWLEDGE	2
SKILL	2

KUXIR97
NAME: FRANCESCO CINQUEMANI
- NO. OF FOLLOWERS: 7,500
- NO. OF VIEWS: 400,000

ABOUT: Pro *Rocket League* player, Let's Player, and streamer Francesco "Kuxir97" Cinquemani is one of three players in Flipsid3 Tactics, one of the highest-ranking pro *Rocket League* teams. The 19-year-old Italian gamer (who records in English) learned all he knows by playing *Supersonic Acrobatic Rocket-Powered Battle-Cars* before getting into *Rocket League*.

HILARIOUSNESS	4
TALKATIVENESS	4
ANGER	1
KNOWLEDGE	3
SKILL	3

STORM RIDERS

HEROES OF THE STORM

Heroes of the Storm is game maker Blizzard's attempt to get in on a piece of the eSports action, sharing many similarities with the likes of *Dota 2* and *League of Legends.* In it you can play as some of the developer's most famous characters from such games as *World of Warcraft* and *StarCraft.*

Released in June 2015, the game has garnered a massive following with millions of players and viewers. While Blizzard doesn't refer to it as a MOBA (it prefers "hero brawler"), it includes many of the genre's key features.

You take control of a hero and, alongside your team, are tasked with destroying the enemy base through fast and fun, lane-based combat. It's tough to master thanks to the tactical gameplay, but check out the players featured here and you'll up your game in no time at all.

DID YOU KNOW?
Heroes of the Storm stars characters from different Blizzard titles, including Overwatch, The Lost Vikings, and Warcraft.

STREAMERS' TOP TIPS

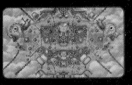

THE DAILY GRIND
Heroes of the Storm regularly prompts you to take part in the daily challenges. Each time you complete a challenge you're rewarded with a few hundred extra pieces of gold.

GOLD NOT MONEY
The game can be quite expensive to play if you spend real money. Instead, try out characters as they rotate weekly, then use the gold you earn playing to unlock them permanently.

TEST RUN
Most people forget that *Heroes of the Storm* includes a Try Before You Buy feature. This means you can play about with characters even when they're not in free rotation.

THE MINI MAP
Be sure to use it as much as you can when playing. It's the best and easiest way to keep track of peripherals, and stay aware of where your enemies, teammates, and objectives are.

BIGGEST LET'S PLAYERS

TOTALBISCUIT

NAME: JOHN BAIN
- NO. OF FOLLOWERS: 2,180,000
- NO. OF VIEWS: 740,000,000

ABOUT: John 'TotalBiscuit' Bain (also known as The Cynical Brit and TotalHalibut) is probably one of the most popular streamers across YouTube and Twitch right now. His speciality is critiquing and explaining new games, but he also likes to bring unknown titles to the attention of gamers. His videos cover a wide range of games and topics. They're educational, but quite critical.

HILARIOUSNESS	
TALKATIVENESS	4
ANGER	3
KNOWLEDGE	4
SKILL	3
	4

MFPALLYTIME

NAME: UNKNOWN
- NO. OF FOLLOWERS: 175,000 ● NO. OF VIEWS: 41,000,000

ABOUT: MFPallytime runs a hugely popular channel that specializes in hero guides, skin showcase videos, and hero strategies. He also posts detailed gameplay videos as soon as a new hero arrives in the game. Plus, he's actually pretty awesome at the game, so both beginner and advanced players can learn something from watching his videos.

HILARIOUSNESS	4
TALKATIVENESS	3
ANGER	3
KNOWLEDGE	4
SKILL	3

KHALDOR TV

NAME: THOMAS KILIAN
- NO. OF FOLLOWERS: 70,000 ● NO. OF VIEWS: 16,000,000

ABOUT: Thomas Kilian has been commentating on the eSports scene for over 14 years, and it's this wealth of experience that elevates his channel from just okay to quite excellent. If you're looking for best-play videos, beginner tutorials, quick tips, hero guides, or *Heroes of the Storm* tournament matches, then you should subscribe to his channel.

HILARIOUSNESS	3
TALKATIVENESS	4
ANGER	3
KNOWLEDGE	4
SKILL	4

KENDRICSWISSH

NAME: KENDRIC SWISSH
- NO. OF FOLLOWERS: 24,000 ● NO. OF VIEWS: 4,500,000

ABOUT: German KendricSwissh is a man of many talents, including eSports commentator and YouTube streamer extraordinaire. His videos focus on *Heroes of the Storm* and other Blizzard titles. His *Epic Plays of the Week* are fun to watch, and, like our other top streamers on here, there are loads of hints, tips, and hero guides ripe for exploration.

HILARIOUSNESS	4
TALKATIVENESS	3
ANGER	2
KNOWLEDGE	4
SKILL	4

SOLID JAKE

NAME: JAKE KULINSKI
- NO. OF FOLLOWERS: 5,600 ● NO. OF VIEWS: 730,000

ABOUT: Jake Kulinski has been involved in eSports for over eight years, and his YouTube channel is a stellar source of tournaments, news, and hero highlights, as well as superbly entertaining podcasts. If you're just starting out on *Heroes of the Storm*, then be sure to check out his *Daily Quest* videos that teach you how to play each hero effectively.

HILARIOUSNESS	2
TALKATIVENESS	3
ANGER	2
KNOWLEDGE	4
SKILL	4

LAURENZSIDE
MEET THE MOST FUN YOUTUBER AROUND!

> I have to keep all my emotions right at the surface when I'm recording.

STARTING OUT

What made you start recording your own YouTube videos?

I had just graduated college with a degree in TV production, and although I was working for a TV company, my position was office-based and not creative at all. After a few months, I started looking for some kind of creative hobby that I could do outside of my job to keep me sane. Meanwhile, I had recently discovered what video-game commentators were on YouTube while searching for footage of the old PS2 game *Fatal Frame 2*. I started noticing that there weren't many girls in this genre, and the ones who were mainly had *Minecraft* or *Call of Duty* channels where they were just trying to be super-cute. One night while I was showing my then-boyfriend—now fiancé—who PewDiePie was, he said, "I've heard you play games before and you sound like him!" Thus, I decided to make a YouTube channel to be that creative hobby I was looking for.

How did you develop your YouTube style?

I was definitely more reserved in my style when I first started, I feel like everyone is. Once I got more comfortable talking to a camera, it was much easier to develop my "YouTube style." If I said or did something that viewers thought was funny, I would continue to do those things again in my videos. Eventually you learn which bits of your personality work best when it comes to YouTube commentating and you then need to build on that. For example, I learned early on that people liked my natural reactions to jump scares, funny game glitches, and not knowing how to play a game well. Thus, I play scary games, glitchy games, and unfamiliar games more often on my channel because they do the best with my YouTube personality.

THE GAMES

How do you decide which games to feature in your YouTube videos?

For me, it's a mixture of three factors: What have my viewers been suggesting I play? What games have other YouTubers been playing that are doing well? What games do I want to play? Sometimes that third factor takes a backseat more than the other two factors, but I really try for it not to. I find that my reactions and expressions are much more natural when I'm playing games I actually want to play, which in turn makes the videos that much better. Also, there are many games I love to play but that don't do well on YouTube because they're either too long or were already played way too much by others. The sweet spot with a game is when all three factors line up perfectly!

How do you change your playstyle?

I definitely always have to be in a more positive mood when I play games for recording versus when I'm not. I tend to not be as talkative if I'm in a bad mood or not feeling well, which obviously doesn't do well for recordings! I also have to amp up my emotions and reactions a bit more to be more animated on camera. That doesn't mean that my reactions are fake *at all*, it just means that they are more apparent than they normally would be. I have to keep all my emotions right at the surface when I'm recording.

Are there games that you won't record?

There are plenty of games I play that I don't record because I don't feel they would do well on YouTube. Long or old games like *Pokémon* I like to play in my spare time but won't stream. There have also been times when I've recorded gameplay where I wasn't happy with the end result and tossed it.

YOUTUBE VIDEOS

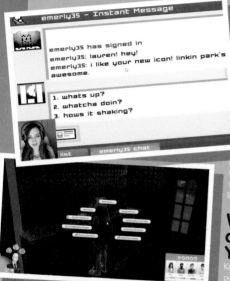

How often do you watch YouTube videos? Do you watch other games, or something else?

I watch YouTube videos every morning while I'm getting ready for work. I also watch them while I'm waiting for my videos to render or for something to load. However, I actually rarely watch other gameplay channels except for my YouTube friends' channels. That's only because I don't want to spoil games for myself that I haven't played yet. I mainly watch vlogging channels, food channels, and lifestyle channels in my spare time.

What's the best thing about being a popular YouTuber?

Knowing I have the power to influence younger people as well as help to brighten their days. I try to be a good role model to kids as much as possible because there are so many bad role models out there. I also love being that constant thing they know will be there when they need a laugh. YouTubers were there for me back before I started a channel, when I was young and needed something to make me smile, it's so amazing getting to be that for other people now.

What's the worst thing?

The stress of creating content. Back before I had a lot of subscribers, I could take a few days off without putting up new videos and not have anyone calling me out for it. Now, if I miss a day, I have people constantly commenting asking where new videos are. It's flattering that they love my content, but it also causes me a lot of stress. Also, stressing over my stats is not fun. If I have a day where I didn't get as many subscribers or views, it bums me out. I know you shouldn't focus on numbers, but it's hard not to sometimes!

DID YOU KNOW? Lauren makes videos about all sorts of games, featuring everything from *The Sims* to *Minecraft*, so you're bound to find something you enjoy!

QUICKFIRE

What is your favorite food of all time?
Bread ... all bread.

What is your favorite music to listen to?
Alternative rock; favourite artist is Incubus.

What's your favorite Twitch emote?
Maybe I'm biased, but my smiling Dexter emote that subscribers get on Twitch is pretty amazing.

What are your hobbies outside of gaming?
Reading, writing, snowboarding, decorating, and binge-watching TV shows.

If you could change

LaurenzSide to any other username possible, what would you change it to?
Pastel_Corgi_Unicorn7

If you had to play one game for the rest of your life, what would it be?
Pokémon Fire Red. It's the original first generation *Pokémon* game but with some much appreciated updates. I could—and have—replayed *Pokémon* over and over since I was a kid and still *love* playing it.

Streamer On...

FIRST-EVER LIVESTREAM

WHO?	REAL NAME?	FANBASE
ZEGOATTT	LAURA SLIVKA	30,000 TWITCH FANS

"It was February 7, 2014. It was Sunday and I was at home, dying from boredom. I had tried to register my account on Twitch for a few weeks but because I had a really old laptop, I had trouble making an account. But this particular evening, the stars aligned because I was trying to make an account and I actually did it! And that was the day of change, when I did my first livestream.

It was absolutely magical. I'm not sure what happened, because at that time I didn't really know how things worked on Twitch, but I think somebody sent viewers to my channel. I remember at one point I had hundreds of viewers and the chat was moving at lightning speed—people commenting on my gameplay, trying to find out who I was, where I was from, and so on. Thinking about it, I realize how lucky I was that so many people discovered my channel on my very first day of streaming, because I was not expecting that!

The quality of my stream was pretty bad. I had a really pixelated stream because my old laptop didn't support HD settings and my camera was awful. You couldn't even see me properly! But it was the beginning of something great. I had the most wonderful experience of growing my channel, and the best community ever."

ZEGOATTT   ZEGOATTT

WHICH KIND OF PLAYER ARE YOU?

Our simple guide will help you find out what type of Twitch streamer or YouTuber you'd be …

START

Do you prefer to play on your own?
— NO
— YES

Do you pick just one game and play it forever?
— NO
— YES

Do you LOVE *Minecraft*?
— NO
— YES

Do you do a lot of funny voices?
— YES
— NO

Do you like specific game genres like action or RPGs?
— NO
— YES

Do you love doing crazy stunts?
— NO
— YES

Do you just play for fun?
— YES
— NO

Are you all about unlocking Achievements?
— YES
— NO

Do you play on any console/format, depending on the game?
— NO
— YES

Do you have to be up-to-date with gaming news?
— NO
— YES

LAID-BACK TEAM PLAYER
Like Stampy, *Minecraft* is your jam! You love everything blocky and you're all about building and adventuring with your friends. You are always happy and you're constantly laughing with your pals!

LOUD AND PROUD
You'll play absolutely anything as long as you're enjoying yourself. Like JackSepticEye, you're full of energy and you can be loud! Whether it's with funny videos or angry shouting, you're quick to express yourself.

MASTER OF ALL
Like DethridgeCraft, you want to play everything! You just want to play as many games as possible, and because you're always the first to the new releases, you'll quickly become a gaming trendsetter.

BRING ON THE CRAZY
Like Markiplier, you're happy whether you're playing on your own or gaming with friends! You're talkative, and while you try to stay positive, sometimes things will get to you and make you scream.

THE CLASSICS NEVER DIE

WORLD OF WARCRAFT

There are very few games that can claim to have had as much success and cultural impact as *World of Warcraft*. While it wasn't the first MMORPG, it is certainly the most famous—and the one that has had the greatest impact on the genre. This is the game that turned Blizzard into a superstar of the video-game world.

Fully launched in 2004, the multiplayer RPG is still going strong today thanks to constant updates and huge expansion packs like *Mists of Pandaria* and *The Wrath of the Lich King*. Even now, new classes like the agile Demon Hunter are being added, giving players a new way to fight through Azeroth with their friends as they try to attain the best gear for their character. When a game allows you to personalize a character or go on epic adventures like *World of Warcraft*, you can understand it's incredible popularity.

DID YOU KNOW?
World of Warcraft is the second-best-selling PC game of all time. Only *Minecraft* has been more successful.

TOP 3 STREAM MOMENTS

LEEROY JENKINS
11 MAY 2005

1 Maybe the most famous moment in streaming history, Leeroy Jenkins shot to fame in 2005. While his party prepared to tackle a tough dungeon, Mr Jenkins decided he'd had enough of talking and hilariously charged into the fray by himself, instantly ruining the team's carefully-laid plan and angering his leader.

SWIFTY CRASHES SERVERS
18 JULY 2011

2 As difficult as it is to believe, a single raiding party managed to crash multiple *WoW* servers. Swifty, featured in our 'Biggest Streamers' section, hosted a gathering online which overloaded servers. While the stunt annoyed many, ultimately it further increased Swifty's notoriety and gained him more fans.

CORRUPTED BLOOD PLAGUE
13 SEPTEMBER 2005

3 One of the new bosses added in patch 1.7, Hakkar, which could infect players with a disease that slowly drained their health… but somehow the disease spread through the entire game world. The panicked outbreak lasted a week and was studied by real-world scientists, before Blizzard eventually stopped the plague.

BIGGEST STREAMERS

TOWELLIEE
NAME: ROBERTO GARCIA
- NO. OF FOLLOWERS: 423,000
- NO. OF VIEWS: 80,400,000

ABOUT: An 11-year *World of Warcraft* veteran, Towelliee actually began his competitive gaming career playing first-person shooters. It wasn't until 2004, when the *WoW* beta became available, that he stepped into the MMO arena. Towelliee is a promoter of the idea that the best way to understand *WoW* is to play slow and absorb everything you see, rather than simply trying to fly toward the max level as quickly as possible.

TALKATIVENESS	4
GAME KNOWLEDGE	
HUMOR	3
SKILL	
AUDIENCE ENGAGEMENT	4

SWIFTY
NAME: JOHN PYLE
- NO. OF FOLLOWERS: 366,000 ● NO. OF VIEWS: 33,800,000

ABOUT: As active on YouTube as he is on Twitch, Swifty is a PvP (Player vs Player) specialist who can be found dealing death and embarrassing less knowledgeable players throughout *WoW*. He has a character in the game named after him: just look for 'John Swifty' in the Ashran region. His streaming setup includes six screens and looks *totally* awesome.

TALKATIVENESS	4
GAME KNOWLEDGE	3
HUMOR	4
SKILL	3
AUDIENCE ENGAGEMENT	4

DUCKSAUCE
NAME: MATTHEW RHODE
- NO. OF FOLLOWERS: 196,000 ● NO. OF VIEWS: 18,500,000

ABOUT: Based in Los Angeles, Ducksauce's streaming success is due to his smooth voice and an ability to never run out of things to say—presumably traits learned in his previous career as an actor. While he's playing *World of Warcraft*, he also does a tremendous job of answering all questions that are asked by his fans.

TALKATIVENESS	
GAME KNOWLEDGE	4
HUMOR	3
SKILL	
AUDIENCE ENGAGEMENT	3

BAJHEERA
NAME: JACKSON BLITON
- NO. OF FOLLOWERS: 255,000 ● NO. OF VIEWS: 17,900,000

ABOUT: As a bodybuilder, Bajheera isn't your usual *World of Warcraft* player—he can certainly claim to being the strongest player in Azeroth! But his Internet fame comes from his deep knowledge of the game as he's been posting *World of Warcraft* videos since starting his YouTube channel back in 2010. There's no better stream for gameplay analysis.

TALKATIVENESS	4
GAME KNOWLEDGE	3
HUMOR	4
SKILL	
AUDIENCE ENGAGEMENT	

CDEWX
NAME: CHARLES DEWLAND
- NO. OF FOLLOWERS: 150,000 ● NO. OF VIEWS: 17,100,000

ABOUT: Part of the Method eSports team, CDEWX has been a professional gamer since 2009, which makes him an industry veteran. He is an elite level PvP performer within *World of Warcraft*, meaning that his stream is essential viewing for anyone seeking to understand how to attack and control real human players.

TALKATIVENESS	3
GAME KNOWLEDGE	
HUMOR	
SKILL	4
AUDIENCE ENGAGEMENT	3

THE CHARACTERS OF THE BIGGEST STARS

STREAMERS' TOP PICKS

ABILITIES

Juggernaut

Enraged Regeneration

Unquenchable Thirst

Storm Bolt

Safeguard

WARRIOR

PLAYER NAME: SWIFTY
PRIMARY ROLE: NIGHT ELF FURY WARRIOR

STATS

STRENGTH	5430
HEALTH	388440
AGILITY	893
STAMINA	6474
SPELL POWER	711

Attack, attack, and more attack is very much the name of the game here. Swifty prefers to load up on talents that buff health, increase speed, and deal out damage in order to maintain a constant barrage of pain. Importantly, spells that decrease cooldown times are also used regularly by Swifty.

ABILITIES

Speed of Light

Fist of Justice

Sacred Shield

Clemency

Holy Avenger

PALADIN

PLAYER NAME: TOWELLIEE
PRIMARY ROLE: DWARF PROTECTION PALADIN

STATS

STRENGTH	6144
HEALTH	573600
AGILITY	451
STAMINA	9560
SPELL POWER	1041

With enormous health reserves and exhaustive levels of stamina, Towelliee's vision of the Paladin is close to what most would consider the perfect blend. Abilities that increase speed, buff protection, and allow for more attacks in a short amount of time only add to its ability to keep itself safe.

STREAMERS' TOP TIPS

DEATH ISN'T SO BAD

CLICK, DON'T TAB

LEARN EVERY CLASS IN PVP

ANALYZE BEFORE QUESTING
Tackling quests in the most efficient way

SHAMAN

PLAYER NAME: CDEWX
PRIMARY ROLE: DWARF ELEMENTAL SHAMAN

STATS

STRENGTH	631
HEALTH	364020
AGILITY	1280
STAMINA	6067
SPELL POWER	6733

A powerful spellcaster, CDEWX's Shaman is loaded with talents that heal itself and those around it. On the flip side, however, the Shaman's low strength rating means that much effort must go into staying as far away as possible from attacking enemies.

ABILITIES

Nature's Guardian

Windwalk Totem

Call of the Elements

Echo of the Elements

Rushing Streams

WARRIOR

PLAYER NAME: BAJHEERA
PRIMARY ROLE: HUMAN FURY WARRIOR

STATS

STRENGTH	5912
HEALTH	394380
AGILITY	889
STAMINA	6573
SPELL POWER	711

Like most Warriors, Bajheera's character's main strengths are its attack power and relentlessness in combat. But Bajheera takes higher risks with the inclusion of spells such as Sudden Death—which gives you the chance to perform an Execute without using any Rage.

ABILITIES

Juggernaut

Enraged Regeneration

Avatar

Sudden Death

Storm Bolt

HUNTER

PLAYER NAME: DUCKSAUCE
PRIMARY ROLE: ORC SURVIVAL HUNTER

STATS

STRENGTH	889
HEALTH	350220
AGILITY	4804
STAMINA	5837
SPELL POWER	851

Speed and accuracy are the Hunter's best friends, and that's exactly what this Orc has. Binding Shot allows him to pin enemies in position, while Posthaste means he can quickly sprint to a new vantage point to fire volleys of arrows. He uses both together for the very best effect.

ABILITIES

Posthaste

Binding Shot

Spirit Bond

Thrill of the Hunt

A Murder of Crows

GUARDIANS OF THE GALAXY

DESTINY

Ever since it burst on to the scene in 2014, *Destiny* has remained one of the highest-rated games among both gamers and critics. Always teasing us with that next bit of gear we need to boost our character's skills, fans have been hooked by the combination of MMO-style looting and slick shooting (developers Bungie also created the *Halo* series). It's super-popular on YouTube;

channels dedicated to *Destiny* playthroughs, humor videos, and tutorials rank among the most-liked and subscribed channels on the site.

Destiny is also popular on Twitch, since fans want to see what sort of gear and strategies other players are using. With expansions such as *The Dark Below* and *The Taken King* keeping it fresh, *Destiny* will be around for a long time to come.

STREAMERS' TOP TIPS

USE THE STORY MODE TO LEVEL UP
"Attempt to find the secret encrypted weapons to wreak havoc," advises HeadCrads. "If you attempt at the earliest level possible to jump in and play against the top players, you're going to have a bad time."

HAVE A BIT OF CLASS
"My first tip for *Destiny* success is to make sure you choose the class that best suits the role you wish to take within *Destiny*," says pro player BennyCentral. The Warlock, Hunter, and Titan classes are all very different, so be sure to choose the right one.

KNOW YOUR MAPS IN THE CRUCIBLE
"Take your time, maneuver around the map, and pick your battles wisely," says TCM pro Marky B. "Otherwise, you may find yourself on the end of a team-shooting exercise and your death will come quicker than you expected."

USE YOUR SUPERS PROPERLY
"As you only get this super-charged every few minutes, save it for a key moment into the game which will benefit yourself and your team the most," advises *Destiny* master FearCrads on using the boosters.

BIGGEST LET'S PLAYERS

DPJ
NAME: DAVID PETER JACKSON
- NO. OF FOLLOWERS: 850,000
- NO. OF VIEWS: 205,000,000

ABOUT: British gamer DPJ has been uploading videos to YouTube since 2008, and over that eight-year period he's built a huge following of fans and subscribers. Over the past few years he's started specializing in *Destiny* content, offering a mixture of top fives, guides, and funny videos. He posts videos on a daily basis to keep fans coming back for more!

HILARIOUSNESS	3
TALKATIVENESS	4
ANGER	3
KNOWLEDGE	3
SKILL	3

MORECONSOLE
NAME: ALAIN ISMAIL
- NO. OF FOLLOWERS: 530,000
- NO. OF VIEWS: 120,000,000

ABOUT: YouTuber MoreConsole joined in 2012, showcasing videos across a variety of games—but it wasn't until the buildup to *Destiny*'s release in 2014 that his channel really started to grow in size. His focus on news updates on everything *Destiny* related has seen him become one of the game's biggest supporters, with over 500,000 subscribers.

HILARIOUSNESS	3
TALKATIVENESS	4
ANGER	1
KNOWLEDGE	4
SKILL	3

DATTO
NAME: STEFAN JONKE
- NO. OF FOLLOWERS: 500,000
- NO. OF VIEWS: 100,500,000

ABOUT: American gamer Datto has been uploading videos and streaming gameplay since 2013, and he is one of the biggest names in *Destiny*-related content. He likes to offer a mixture of video types, including news updates, commentaries, and gameplay tips. He does a lot of his streaming via YouTube to keep all his content in the same place.

HILARIOUSNESS	2
TALKATIVENESS	3
ANGER	2
KNOWLEDGE	4
SKILL	4

PLANETDESTINY
NAME: UNKNOWN
- NO. OF FOLLOWERS: 480,000
- NO. OF VIEWS: 120,000,000

ABOUT: This team of YouTubers comes together every weekday to create new videos, from podcasts about the latest *Destiny* news to online gameplay. They have a regular schedule, so you can always get more of your favorite videos, but the best part is that these guys really know what they're talking about—perfect for true *Destiny* fans.

HILARIOUSNESS	3
TALKATIVENESS	5
ANGER	2
KNOWLEDGE	5
SKILL	4

KING GOTHALION
NAME: TRAVIS LOFLAND
- NO. OF FOLLOWERS: 270,000
- NO. OF VIEWS: 45,000,000

ABOUT: King Gothalion is easily one of the funniest streaming *Destiny* players. His videos cover many different genres, including action-RPGs, MMOs, shooters, and mobile games, but *Destiny* is easily one of his favorites. He usually keeps YouTube for news updates for the games, while making Twitch his main platform for gameplay and events.

HILARIOUSNESS	5
TALKATIVENESS	5
ANGER	3
KNOWLEDGE	4
SKILL	3

CAN YOU DIG IT?

TERRARIA

There's a lot to learn about *Terraria*, and plenty of tools to familiarize yourself with before you jump into its massive, colorful world. But that's what the most popular Let's Players do best—folks like Stampy give out funny, simple advice to their millions of subscribers. If you need to know how to mine, build a house or even pronounce the word "Terraria," YouTube is where to go.

If you like *Minecraft*, you'll love *Terraria*, because the two games are surprisingly similar. They're both about exploring, mining resources, building, and fighting off scary monsters, but *Terraria* does it in a side-scrolling world. You'll soon see that *Terraria*'s world contains more weapons, enemies, and bosses than *Minecraft*; it takes a lot of courage to be a hero in this 2D realm!

DID YOU KNOW?
The most players simultaneously playing *Terraria* on Steam at one time was 159,175, recorded in July 2015.

TOP 3 LET'S PLAY MOMENTS

CHRISTMAS SPECIAL!
DECEMBER 25, 2015

1 Fighting off monsters and searching for chunks of ore is the main part of playing *Terraria*, but there's nothing like coming back to your own house for a rest. On Christmas morning, ChimneySwift and his pals did just that. After spending months perfecting their base, they topped it off with a big ol' Christmas tree.

MY FIRST NIGHT
MARCH 27, 2013

2 Stampy's one of the nicest, sweetest Let's Players around, so watching him get chewed up by Little Eaters and Eaters of Souls on his very first night in *Terraria* is a little heartbreaking. But also funny. "Leave me alone! I've not even built my house yet!" It goes to show how much you need to be prepared to survive!

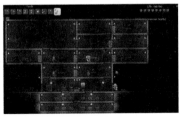

NOODLES
JULY 4, 2015

3 RockLeeSmile is still up-and-coming in the Let's Play world, but when it comes to *Terraria*, he's a pro. What's cool is that he's got a sense of humor, too. In this episode, he finishes building his masterpiece, an enormous house in the shape of the tower from the DC television series *Teen Titans*.

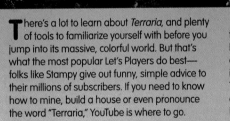

BIGGEST LET'S PLAYERS

CHIPPYGAMING
NAME: JAMES BENNETT
- NO. OF FOLLOWERS: 230,000
- NO. OF VIEWS: 40,000,000

ABOUT: Chippy started his channel when he was just 14 and has been posting regular *Terraria* videos ever since. Now all grown up, he recently moved to a bigger, newer office so he could continue to work on his channel full-time and make it brighter and better. As well as standard playthroughs, his channel showcases *Terraria* "Life Hacks," simple little tips to help you find the best ore and easily defeat enemies. There are over 100 of them, so you're likely to find something helpful!

HILARIOUSNESS	3
TALKATIVENESS	3
ANGER	2
KNOWLEDGE	4
SKILL	4

MEETYOURDEMIZE
NAME: UNKNOWN ● NO. OF FOLLOWERS: 145,000 ● NO. OF VIEWS: 30,000,000

ABOUT: MeetYourDemize is all about tutorials, tips and guides on how to unlock the latest armor, hooks, and other items for your own *Terraria* hero. He explains exactly what you need to acquire for each upgrade and talks through how to get them, making his videos a brilliant source of information for newcomers and experienced players alike.

HILARIOUSNESS	3
TALKATIVENESS	
ANGER	1
KNOWLEDGE	
SKILL	4

STAMPY
NAME: JOSEPH GARRETT ● NO. OF FOLLOWERS: 7,300,000 ● NO. OF VIEWS: 5,000,000,000

ABOUT: Stampy started making videos after he'd finished college, leaving his job to follow his dream full-time. His character is often joined by Sqaishey Quack, played by Stampy's girlfriend, Bethany. In addition to stories set around Cat and Quack, and missions that he sets himself, his *Terraria* videos offer viewers challenges to complete in the game.

HILARIOUSNESS	5
TALKATIVENESS	5
ANGER	0
KNOWLEDGE	2
SKILL	3

CHIMNEYSWIFT11
NAME: UNKNOWN ● NO. OF FOLLOWERS: 1,900,000 ● NO. OF VIEWS: 510,000,000

ABOUT: ChimneySwift is one of the most popular Let's Players, with a fan base that is now almost 2 million—affectionately called the "Swifters." He started his channel in 2011 and within just one year he had 200,000 subscribers. His videos are friendly and welcoming, but he knows his stuff, too, and he always gets super-excited about new *Terraria* updates.

HILARIOUSNESS	4
TALKATIVENESS	5
ANGER	1
KNOWLEDGE	3
SKILL	3

ROCKLEESMILE
NAME: NICK REINEKE ● NO. OF FOLLOWERS: 85,000 ● NO. OF VIEWS: 17,300,000

ABOUT: RockLeeSmile is still making a name for himself in the busy world of YouTube, but if you check out his videos, you'll soon understand why he's one of the best *Terraria* Let's Players around. From his cool weapon tutorials to his brave adventures into the difficult realms, RockLeeSmile is a *Terraria* pro, and the go-to guy when you need expert tips.

HILARIOUSNESS	2
TALKATIVENESS	5
ANGER	0
KNOWLEDGE	5
SKILL	5

STAT ATTACK

7.5 Million
players at
peak time

130
champions
to choose
from

852 / 85
384 / 38

149,508
HP damage dealt
by Master Yi
all time

2 ^{vs} 1   1/0/0   26   07:28

FPS: 16   40 ms

TimmyShire

5

LEAGUE OF LEGENDS

IN NO DANGER of losing its spot as the world's most popular streamed game, fans watch over 90 million hours of *League of Legends* every month on Twitch. Need more proof? The massive *League of Legends* World Championship Series 2015 accumulated 360 million hours of live eSports viewed!

LUCIAN
is the most
popular
champion

16   F

1   2   3   4   2

5   6   7   B

1571

THE WORLD'S FASTEST GAMERS

SPEEDRUNNERS

What is a speedrunner? Exactly what you might think it is—someone who tries to complete a game as quickly as possible! Whether it's using their vast knowledge, smart glitches or clever tricks you haven't thought of, there are various different types of speedruns out there. The traditional ones are about getting to the end of the game as quickly as possible but other speedruns involve completing the game to 100 percent along the way (getting all the stars in *Super Mario 64*, for example). Another popular type of speedrun is the tool-assisted speedrun, where the player programs the game to do things that aren't possible by a human. Whether it's a traditional speedrun, a 100 percent speedrun or tool-assisted, every player must show off an impressive in-depth knowledge of the game—that's what makes them such great fun to watch!

DID YOU KNOW?
One more attainable world record is Green Hill Zone Act 1 for *Sonic the Hedgehog*—the record is 25 seconds!

TOP **3** STREAM MOMENTS

THREE MEGA MAN GAMES AT THE SAME TIME
DECEMBER 9, 2012

1 Completing one *Mega Man* game is tricky enough … but using tool assists (programmed moves that allow for precision), Japanese player agwawaf manages to complete *three Mega Man* games at the same time, all using exactly the same moves.

THE FASTEST TIME IN THE WORLD FOR MARIO
JANUARY 15, 2016

2 *Super Mario Bros.* is still the gold standard for speedruns. Darbian has set the most recent world record of 4:57.427 for whizzing through the game. Incredibly, darbian suggests that record could be further improved, since he lost some time in the water section of world.

BLINDFOLDED GAMER GETS VERY, VERY CONFUSED
AUGUST 30, 2014

3 25 hours into a blindfolded speedrun of *Ocarina of Time*, 808Tokyoboi somehow stumbled on a new glitch and clipped above the map, ending up in an area he'd never been to before. Cue Tokyoboi trying to figure out what's happened, while blindfolded and very confused!

BIGGEST SPEEDRUNNERS

SIGLEMIC

MICHAEL SIGLER
- NO. OF FOLLOWERS: **115,000**
- NO. OF VIEWS: **20,000,000**

ABOUT: One of the legendary speedrunners, Siglemic has conquered *Super Mario 64* in every way—straight up speedruns, with a certain amount of stars, with all the stars and so on. Siglemic now plays games like *StarCraft II* but still returns to *Super Mario 64*, showing off dazzling tricks and glitches to blitz through the game.

HILARIOUSNESS	2
TALKATIVENESS	2
ANGER	2
KNOWLEDGE	3
SKILL	5

THEMEXICANRUNNER

NAME: UNKNOWN
- NO. OF FOLLOWERS: **35,000**
- NO. OF VIEWS: **3,400,000**

ABOUT: TheMexicanRunner has stamped his authority on all sorts of NES games, from *Super Off Road* to *Hook*. His dedication to beating games has meant that he's cracked some games open under speedrunning conditions as well, but if you want to see obscure games played well, TheMexicanRunner should be your first port of call!

HILARIOUSNESS	3
TALKATIVENESS	4
ANGER	2
KNOWLEDGE	3
SKILL	2

PJ

NAME: PJ DICESARE
- NO. OF FOLLOWERS: **18,000**
- NO. OF VIEWS: **1,100,000**

ABOUT: Despite the skill demands involved with becoming a prolific speedrunner, PJ is extremely laid-back. He zeroes in on NES and SNES games like *ActRaiser* and *Bionic Commando*, and plays a range of modern games on his stream as well. Whether it's seeing a game being broken apart by a top player or just a fun time, check him out!

HILARIOUSNESS	2
TALKATIVENESS	2
ANGER	1
KNOWLEDGE	2
SKILL	4

TASMALLEO

NAME: UNKNOWN
- NO. OF FOLLOWERS: **1,084**
- NO. OF VIEWS: **4,000**

ABOUT: What makes TAS Malleo's tool-assisted speedruns worth watching are his excellent commentary throughout. Considered, smart and insightful, he explains all the clever tricks and glitches used to speed through the games. His *Paper Mario: Thousand Year Door* speedrun is especially interesting …

HILARIOUSNESS	1
TALKATIVENESS	3
ANGER	1
KNOWLEDGE	5
SKILL	4

ZFG1

NAME: UNKNOWN
- NO. OF FOLLOWERS: **64,000**
- NO. OF VIEWS: **5,900,000**

ABOUT: ZFG1, or ZeldaFreakGlitcha, is one of the most prolific *Zelda* speedrunners on the Web. His YouTube channel is full of complete runs, along with shorter clips showing off the quickest ways to beat individual sections. He often streams these speedruns, so you can watch him playing through games live and he'll answer questions from the chat.

HILARIOUSNESS	2
TALKATIVENESS	3
ANGER	1
KNOWLEDGE	4
SKILL	5

MASTER GAMING JARGON

ETA
An unfinished version of a game that's released early to a small group of players so the developers can learn about any glitches or bugs they need to fix before releasing the final game to the world.

CARRY
In MOBAs, a character that has to be "carried" by the rest of the team while they spend time collecting items and gaining levels, until late in the game when their powerful abilities will help totally dominate the opposition.

CHARACTER SKIN
A different outfit, or even a completely different look for a character that can be unlocked or bought using in-game currency or real-world money.

CHAT
A live text feed that can be used by viewers, or the streamer, to communicate with each other and express opinions on the stream. Usually full of emotes and references to memes.

CLAN
A group of players who stick together in-game to achieve a common goal. This is commonly seen in MMOs, where players have to join up to beat the tougher bosses.

CLUTCH
Used to describe a successful play at a critical moment in competitive gaming, usually determining the outcome of the game. Clutch victories will often refer to one player taking out the whole opposition team in one powerful manuever.

COSPLAY
Shortened from "costume play," this is when video-game fans dress up as their favorite characters in real life.

EDITOR/ED
People working on a stream behind the scenes, who can run commercials and create highlights while the stream is still happening.

EMOTE
Small images that can be added to the chat window by typing a specific phrase. Subscribers to a channel can access custom emotes for the chat.

GG
Good Game. Used extensively in MOBAs after each round, but can be used in any game.

HIGH LEVEL
A term used to describe gameplay by skilled players. Gameplay in tournaments is

often referred to as "high-level play," for example.

JUNGLER

A player who stays in the area between lanes (see "Lane" entry) in MOBA games.

KAPPA

An emote used in twitch.tv's chat to denote sarcasm. It is the face of Josh Kappa, an early employee at Twitch.

LAG

The term used to describe a noticeable delay between the player's commands and the actions occurring on-screen—usually caused by a poor Internet connection.

LET'S PLAY

A video showing gameplay footage, with live commentary recorded over the top of the game itself while the person is playing. Massively popular on YouTube.

MECH

A term used to described robots that vaguely resemble humans (they will often have two arms, two legs and a head) and are often used for combat purposes.

MMORPG:

Stands for "massively multiplayer online role-playing game." These are RPGs that thousands of people can play online at the same time, such as *World of Warcraft* or *DC Universe Online*.

MOBA

Stands for "multiplayer online battle arena." Players are tasked with destroying an enemy base while protecting their own. Normally there are one to three "lanes" through which players

PVP

Player Versus Player. Typically used in MMORPGs, but also applies to shooters, this pits players against each another in a competitive match, rather than playing against AI (Artificial Intelligence) enemies.

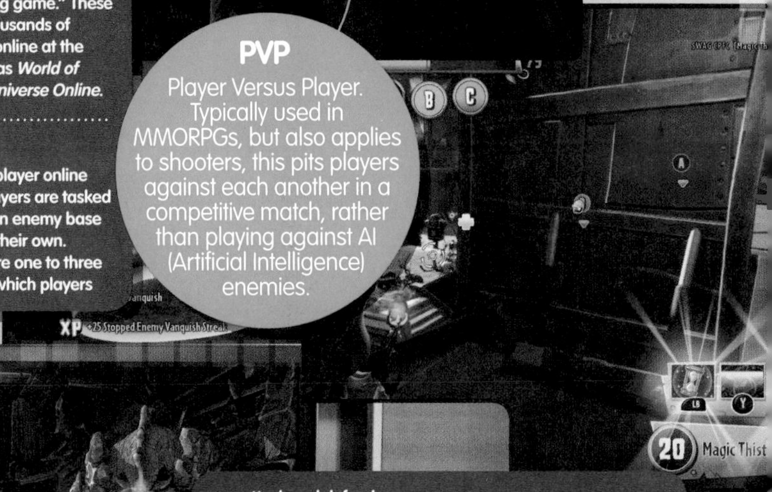

LANE

Name given to the main areas of attack and defense in MOBA games, where the map is split into top, middle and bottom lanes. A hero is assigned to each lane to attack and defend.

PVE

Player versus Environment. Most typically used in MMORPGs, this means players versus computer-controlled enemies rather than versus other players. Usually, PvE can be played alone and contains some sort of storyline.

can attack and defend, as well as a "jungle," which contains creatures that can be killed for more experience.

MODS

Short for "modifications," which are often small programs you download that change games slightly, such as multiplayer mods for *Minecraft*. These tend to be for PC games only since console games don't allow for mods.

PARTNER

Can refer to another streamer who shares a channel, or may be a company or product that the streamer advertises while they play.

SHOUTCASTING

A term used to describe the commentary on a livestream or live eSport game.

STEAM

A popular gaming platform on PC that allows you to buy games, then play them with other friends online and earn achievements within the Steam ecosystem.

TIMEOUT

A less severe version of a ban on Twitch. Timeouts may last for any amount of time from a few minutes to several days, and too many timeouts will usually result in a permanent ban from the streamer in question.

TWITCH

A website that allows users to watch people streaming gameplay live. The site contains a comments system that lets you speak to the streamer and other watchers, and follow channels you like.